Understanding Reddit

This book offers a comprehensive scholarly overview of Reddit, one of the most popular and least studied social platforms of the early 21st century.

The book inspires new ways of thinking about Reddit, considering it from multiple perspectives: through a historical lens, as a site where identity is forged, as a democracy, as a community, and as a news aggregator and distributor. By bringing theories from computer-mediated communication, communication studies, and sociology to bear on original, large-scale observational analyses of Reddit's communities, this book provides a uniquely comprehensive overview of the platform's first 15 years. Understanding Reddit will help us make sense of how rapidly growing communities function in an era of mass online anonymity.

Serving both as a primer on how social behavior on Reddit plays out, and as a way of locating it within multiple theoretical traditions, the book will offer important insights to scholars and students in the disciplines of communication, media studies, information science, internet and emerging media studies, and sociology.

Elliot T. Panek studies the uses and effects of digital media from sociological and psychological perspectives. He has published research on the social dynamics of online communities, media addiction, and media use and political polarization. He is an Associate Professor at the University of Alabama.

Routledge Focus on Digital Media and Culture

The *Serial* Podcast and Storytelling in the Digital Age
Edited by Ellen McCracken

Media Piracy in the Cultural Economy
Intellectual Property and Labor Under Neoliberal Restructuring
Gavin Mueller

Mobilizing the Latinx Vote
Media, Identity, and Politics
Arthur D. Soto-Vásquez

Playlisting
Collecting Music, Remediated
Onur Sesigür

Understanding Reddit
Elliot T. Panek

Algorithms and Subjectivity
The Subversion of Critical Knowledge
Eran Fisher

Understanding Reddit

Elliot T. Panek

Routledge
Taylor & Francis Group
LONDON AND NEW YORK

First published 2022
by Routledge
2 Park Square, Milton Park, Abingdon, Oxon OX14 4RN

and by Routledge
605 Third Avenue, New York, NY 10158

Routledge is an imprint of the Taylor & Francis Group, an informa business

British Library Cataloguing-in-Publication Data
A catalogue record for this book is available from the British Library

Library of Congress Cataloging-in-Publication Data
Names: Panek, Elliot T., author.
Title: Understanding Reddit / Elliot T. Panek.
Description: Abingdon, Oxon ; New York, NY : Routledge, 2022. | Includes bibliographical references and index.
Identifiers: LCCN 2021044119 (print) | LCCN 2021044120 (ebook) |
Subjects: LCSH: Reddit (Firm) | Online social networks. | Computer bulletin boards. | Online chat groups. | Internet—Social aspects.
Classification: LCC HM743.R447 P36 2022 (print) | LCC HM743.R447 (ebook) | DDC 302.30285—dc23/eng/20211110
LC record available at https://lccn.loc.gov/2021044119
LC ebook record available at https://lccn.loc.gov/2021044120

ISBN: 978-0-367-71419-2 (hbk)
ISBN: 978-0-367-71422-2 (pbk)
ISBN: 978-1-003-15080-0 (ebk)

DOI: 10.4324/9781003150800

Typeset in Times New Roman
by codeMantra

Contents

Figures

Acknowledgments

Much of the research and many of the ideas in this book come from my work with the Alabama Reddit Research Group at the University of Alabama. For the past six years, I've been incredibly fortunate to work with diligent, creative students, fellow faculty, and researchers on a passion project. The abilities and perspectives of this group shaped what I know about Reddit, and I am indebted to them for their contributions: Naiyan Jones, Wyatt Harrison, Jue Hou, Connor Hollenbach, Rebecca Britt, Jinjie Yang, Matthew Gaines, and Tyler Rhodes. I also would like to thank my teachers and mentors for giving me the intellectual foundation that informs how I approach any topic of study: W. Russell Neuman, L. Rowell Heusmann, Joseph Straubhaar, and Sharon Strover. Thank you to my editor Suzanne Richardson at Routledge for having faith in this project. Thank you to my colleagues at the University of Alabama for helping me through the process of writing my first book: Andy Billings, Cory Armstrong, Jeremy Butler, Jessica Maddox, Cynthia Peacock, and Matthew Barnidge. Thank you to my fellow International Communication Association members for stimulating conversations and inspiring research about media technologies: Bree McEwan, Nick Bowman, Catalina Toma, Joe Bayer, Adrienne Massanari, and Anna Gibson. Thank you to my students – the ideas you present in your writing and in class discussions are as much a part of my thinking on any topic as the books and articles I read. Thank you to my friends and family, particularly my mother and father for cultivating my curiosity from an early age. And thank you to my wife, Kathryn, for being so supportive, patient, and encouraging, and for the enlightening dinner conversations about what we saw on Reddit that day.

1 What is Reddit?

Over its first 15 years, Reddit achieved an unusual kind of popularity. It was as widely used as well-known social media platforms like Twitter (Redditinc.com, 2021) but members of the general public would often claim only to know *of* it rather than know how it worked or what, exactly, it was. The general public's knowledge drew largely from news coverage of several high-profile instances in which coordinated actions of hundreds of thousands of Reddit users jumped off the platform and disrupted reality: the misidentification of the Boston Marathon bomber; the coalescing of support for then-U.S. Presidential candidate Donald Trump; stock market volatility precipitated by the day traders of r/wallstreetbets. What is Reddit doing when it's not making headlines? How does the whole of Reddit – that vast ecosystem of online communities hosting the largest conversations in the history of humanity – function?

The purpose of this book is to help scholars, researchers, students, and anyone with an interest in online communities and social media understand Reddit better. For those already familiar with Reddit, the book is intended to inspire new ways of thinking about it. It is chiefly concerned with design and user behavior in the aggregate. It does not treat Reddit as an abstraction or as an unchanging object with a significance or meaning that can be interpreted, but rather as the sum of the actions taken by designers and users over its first 15 years viewed through several prisms.

The first two chapters view Reddit from historical perspectives. Chapter 2 sketches out a brief history of Reddit and its subreddits, and Chapter 3 locates the platform in the history and evolving cultures of the internet. Each subsequent chapter corresponds to a way of understanding Reddit *as* something: a venue in which identity is expressed and understood (Chapter 4), a democracy (Chapter 5), a community (Chapter 6), a news aggregator (Chapter 7), and a place (Chapter 8).

DOI: 10.4324/9781003150800-1

These aren't so much discrete theoretical perspectives as metaphors that connect us to a wealth of insight and experience in thinking about group behavior.

If you've opened this book, it is assumed that you have some interest in or curiosity about Reddit. It is not assumed that you have any particular level of knowledge or familiarity with it. Readers may have spent thousands of hours on Reddit or may have only heard of Reddit but never used it. To establish a foundation of knowledge on which the rest of the book will build and to create a common starting point, this chapter answers some basic questions about Reddit: what it is, why it exists, and how it works.

Reddit as content sorter

To know Reddit, it is important to know something about the online information environment in which it arose. Reddit and its precursors, like Digg and del.icio.us, addressed a problem that accompanied the explosion of user-generated content at the turn of the century. Specifically, there was no means by which internet users could easily sort appealing or useful content from unappealing or useless content. In the earliest days of the internet, websites deemed appealing or useful by particular users were often already known to those users, in the way that niche magazines or cable channels were known to their target audiences. The paradigm for encountering content on the web was inscribed in the name of the tool used to navigate it: the web *browser*. One browsed websites as one browsed magazines on a rack or books on a shelf. Somewhat similarly, the term "web surfing," adapted from television "channel surfing," implied an activity that bore fruit as long as the options remained somewhat limited.

With the rapid growth of the online content universe, it became likelier that many bits of worthy content would go unnoticed. This vast amount of information needed sorting. Search engines such as Google addressed this need, but only when users had a clear idea of what they sought. Google worked so well and scaled up with the rapid expansion of the internet, largely because it ranked websites based on how web users behaved rather than by imposing a static, "top-down" system of categorization. Web pages appearing in a search were ranked based on how many other websites linked to the page. But if internet users sought something more general, if they approached the web in the way that they were accustomed to approaching the television – seeking entertainment, edification, or mere distraction – search engines were of less use. This was in part because the value of entertainment content was so fleeting; a bit of content may be appealing or relevant for a day, but its appeal or relevancy decayed before web page creators bothered to link to it. This kind of sorting needed to rely on a lower-effort user behavior, something more casual than link-making.

News aggregation software (e.g., "Rich Site Summary" or RSS feeds) offered users the ability to "subscribe" to news websites and blogs, reducing the torrent of potentially appealing content to a manageable, personalized pipeline of short summaries similar to a repertoire of preferred cable channels. Social bookmarking sites such as del.icio.us relied on a large number of users' active choices (i.e., "folksonomies"), allowing them to assemble lists of weblinks and thereby crowdsource the job of content curation. As effective as these tools were, the lists they yielded tended to be comprised of links to entire websites (e.g., *The New York Times*) rather than particular web pages or discrete bits of content (e.g., a news article, or a picture). The "news aggregation" approach to content curation became less tenable as social media platforms and image hosting sites such as Twitter and TinyPic further atomized the online content universe.

It was in this context that Reddit came to be. Reddit belonged to a class of websites known as "social news websites." From the beginning, this was a misnomer: social news websites aggregated links to more than just news stories. Despite the inadequacy of the label with regard to content type, the word "news" reflected the way users consumed content through these sites: with a kind of endless appetite for novelty and/or current-ness. The constant replenishment of novel content is at the heart of many popular social media platforms' appeal and, in part, the reason why they displace traditional news outlets in the media diets of some internet users. This replenishment is made possible by registered users' ability to easily submit new links to Reddit, colloquially known as "posts." These posts are then collectively sorted by an even-lower-effort user behavior: voting. When many users click the "upvote" button next to a post, the post climbs up the list; clicking the "downvote" button causes the post to fall toward the bottom. In this manner, registered Reddit users collectively determine both the content and each bit of content's level of prominence or visibility.

If the rapid rate at which the online universe expanded is Reddit's *raison d'etre*, it has also presented continual challenges relating to information and community management. One trait that allowed the platform to deal with those challenges, one that set it apart from popular social networking sites like Twitter and Facebook, is its modularity. Instead of having a single list of posts, Reddit divides posts into topic-based lists, or "subreddits." These subreddit designations were, at first, a way to organize content, but later became the basis for customizing the user experience. Registered Reddit users assemble lists of posts they see on their homepages by subscribing to or "joining" particular subreddits.

Personalization is a defining characteristic of networked digital media. The centrality of this attribute to communication technology design is counterbalanced by a deep-seated human desire to know what is popular, not necessarily so as to adopt popular preferences as one's own but instead to survey one's social environment. Trending topics on social media platforms and "most read" news articles speak to this desire, distilling and distorting public opinion into easily consumable lists. Collectively vetted lists are heuristics for determining the potential value of content to the user, but they are also valuable social information.

The complicated history of Reddit's default homepage – what unregistered users see when they visit the site – speaks to this tension between users' desire for further personalization of the web and the need to know what is popular. As the self-proclaimed "front page of the internet," Reddit sought to strike a balance among the same forces that shape information flows on news and social networking websites: popular consensus, editorial choice, opaque algorithm. During Reddit's early stages of development, a list of default subreddits was chosen by Reddit administrators (administrators are paid employees of Reddit). This allowed administrators to highlight the diversity of subreddit topics by adding less popular ones to the default homepage while hiding popular subreddits that might be off-putting to newcomers. This interventionalist approach to curation ran counter to the perception of Reddit as a democracy (see Chapter 5), though it likely shaped the userbase during a period of significant growth by attracting a more diverse group of internet users than a pure popularity ranking of posts would have yielded. Reddit replaced the homepage drawn from administrator-selected subreddits with a list of posts ranked by an algorithm (u/daniel, 2018). The algorithm takes into account the number of votes accrued by a post and the speed at which the upvotes were accrued, but also takes into account another of Reddit's core components: the comments.

Reddit as a site of discourse

The presence of user-generated commentary sets Reddit apart from predecessors solely focused on content aggregation and sorting. Many Reddit users, now and throughout Reddit's history, do not engage with this commentary in any meaningful way, choosing to use Reddit only as a means of content sorting. But for millions of other users, reading and posting comments are central to the Reddit experience. Nearly all popular posts on the site have comments, often thousands of comments per post. In some cases (called "self-posts"), posts contain no links to other web pages but are only statements or questions intended to spark conversation (e.g., "What would you like to confess?").

Online exchanges among those who have not met face-to-face date back to the earliest days of the internet. At that time, groups participating in online discourse tended to be relatively small and homogeneous, consisting of tech-savvy individuals who returned repeatedly to the sites of discourse. Regardless of whether these interactions, which lacked certain characteristics that were part and parcel to face-to-face interactions (e.g., social cues and accountability), generated something tantamount to "community" (see Chapter 6), they occurred at a small enough scale that the exchanges resembled what is commonly thought of as conversation.

Here again, rapid growth of internet use in the early 21st century presented a challenge: how to keep online exchanges among thousands of users from becoming a list of disconnected statements; people shouting into an anonymous void, failing to connect. Reddit addresses this challenge with two design features. It applies the voting system it uses on posts to its comments, allowing registered users to collectively sort them. Additionally, Reddit allows its users to publicly reply to comments, to reply to replies, to reply to *those* replies, *ad infinitum*, yielding a branching structure of commentary. While imperfect for a variety of reasons discussed in subsequent chapters, these features have created a discourse that, at least at times, more closely resembles conversation than a list of disconnected thoughts. Comments on a given Reddit post are not unlike the smaller-scale conversations that have filled message boards and online chat rooms since the dawn of the internet: a mix of helpful, hurtful, and often humorous exchanges among strangers.

Though these design features have allowed Reddit to preserve some of the conversational feel of earlier, smaller-scale online discourse, the voting mechanism affects qualities of discourse in important ways. Voting allows the funniest, pithiest, or most insightful comments to rise to the top while the unfunny, un-pithy, un-insightful comments that tend to clog up most large-scale online conversations sink below a threshold of visibility. This yields conversations that are often as entertaining and appealing as the posts that link to other web pages. Two subreddits comprised entirely of self-posts – r/AskReddit and r/IAmA – are consistently among the most popular. Like the voting system for posts, the result of this method of sorting comments is only as good as the people behind it; it reflects a collective sensibility more than a platonic ideal of quality.

User roles

Reddit users occupy a variety of roles on the platform: *administrators ("admins"); moderators ("mods")*; registered users who post or comment, heretofore referred to in this book as "*contributors*"; registered users who vote on comments or posts, heretofore referred to as *constituents*; and *visitors*. These roles are hierarchical – administrators have more power than moderators, who have more power than contributors, constituents, or visitors to affect the content and discourse of Reddit. The design of this hierarchy was based on earlier forms of online group communication such as Internet Relay Chat (IRC) in which the duties of community moderation were delegated to a select group of users while administrators dedicated their time to technical upkeep of the site or platform (u/KeyserSosa, 2010). Though "administrators" and "moderators" are titles used within Reddit, "contributors," "constituents," and "visitors" are not; these titles are used in this book merely to explicate differences among users in terms of their engagement with the platform.

Administrators, who are most often paid employees of the site, design and maintain the website's infrastructure, interface, and other site-wide features. Like most websites, Reddit has undergone numerous re-designs over its first 15 years, though they have been less drastic than those undergone by most websites of comparable size over such a long time period. Digg, a popular social news website that lost a sizable number of users to Reddit following a re-design, provided a cautionary tale about the perils of "top-down" intervention. Perhaps out of a fear of instigating a similar mass exodus, Reddit has made relatively minor, infrequent changes to its design while allocating the power to set rules governing acceptable content to subreddit moderators.

Unlike administrators, moderators are unpaid volunteers motivated by an interest in the subreddit topic and a kind of civic-mindedness (Matias, 2019; Seering et al., 2019), though those who are critical of moderators often attribute to them a desire for authority. Creators of subreddits are appointed as moderators by default, adding additional moderators in an ad hoc fashion to keep up with subreddit growth. The process by which new moderators are added is opaque and inconsistent across subreddits.

Moderators set the rules and make modifications to the functionality of their subreddits. Unlike other popular social media platforms that implement content rules across the entire platform, Reddit's modularity allows moderators to customize rules. For example, moderators may stipulate that contributors avoid personally attacking others, or they may require users to have a minimum amount of experience on the platform (e.g., an account that is at least one year old) before they contribute to the subreddit. Moderators can use automated programs or "bots" to automatically remove posts that violate a rule or automatically post an encouraging message of welcome to newcomers (Matias, Simko, & Reddan, 2020). If moderators find that a contributor has violated a rule, they have the power to ban the contributor and remove their post or comment. There is no single norm in terms of the ways in which moderators intervene to shape the content and character of their subreddits (Gibson, 2019; Matias, 2019).

Most of the work of moderators is unglamorous and invisible: removing spam posted by advertisers, keeping discussions on topic, creating and maintaining a list of frequently asked questions, and (particularly in the early stages of a subreddit) generating discussion and promoting interest in the subreddit. Such work is not unlike the volunteer labor of moderators of earlier online discussion boards (Collins & Berge, 1997; Preece, 2000) or regular contributors to Wikipedia (Kriplean, Beschastnikh, & McDonald, 2008). As in other online forums, subreddit moderators make choices affecting exclusion of unwanted members or content, organize information, and set norms (Grimmelmann, 2015), though their choices are limited by the design and functionality of the platform.

Contributors are Reddit users who post or comment but possess no special privileges or abilities to set or enforce rules on Reddit or within any subreddit. Though administrators posted some of the very first posts on Reddit and moderators often "seed" their subreddits with posts, contributors generate the bulk of the content on Reddit. Contributors' submissions may include a link to a web page, a statement or question intended to initiate discussion, or an original creative work. This range of creative labor associated with contributions – references to work created by others, original commentary, one's own creative work – is indicative of a blurred distinction between creation and re-distribution (i.e., "sharing") commonly seen following the rise of websites, applications, and platforms that relied on user-generated content (Bruns, 2007). Those who comment on Reddit also contribute to its content, though comments are not as prominent as posts; a user must click on the post and scroll down to see comments.

Constituents are registered users who upvote or downvote posts or comments. These users may or may not contribute posts or comments, but their votes determine the visibility of others' posts and comments, and thus shape content and discourse on the platform.

Visitors contribute neither posts nor comments and are distinct from constituents in that they do not vote on posts or comments. Visitors to Reddit must create an account and select a username in order to subscribe to certain subreddits and thus curate the content they see. Unregistered visitors can access most of the content on Reddit (certain subreddits are "private" and can only be accessed by moderators or, in some cases, users who subscribe to or join the subreddits), but they experience the platform as information consumers. Such users of online participatory platforms have long been referred to as "lurkers," a term many see as unfairly pejorative. Visitors on Reddit, like their counterparts on other online communities, have a variety of motivations for not posting or commenting, including privacy, not feeling as though they have anything worthy or relevant to contribute, being more interested in information gathering and entertainment than being social, or simply not having the time to contribute (Nonnecke & Preece, 1999). As is the case with many online communities, visitors outnumber contributors on Reddit.

Karma

Aside from usernames, all registered Reddit users have another datum attached to their account: a karma score. This number roughly corresponds to numbers of total upvotes the user's posts and comments have garnered. Just as upvotes are a convenient metric of the popularity of posts or comments, karma score is a metric of a user's ability to generate popular posts or comments.

To understand precisely what is communicated by karma score, it is useful to compare this metric to one employed by several popular social media platforms: the number of followers. On platforms in which users encounter other users' posts primarily by following those users, the number of followers indicates the number of people who like the posts, but also the number *exposed* to the posts (i.e., audience size). Followers, like subscribers, are a kind of captive audience, exposed to another user's content by default. Reddit users who happened to like a contributor's post are not any more likely to encounter the contributor's content in the future. The result of this difference is a different relationship between popularity and influence, and the ease with which popularity within a platform can be commodified. While an

Instagram user with a large number of followers can promise to deliver a large audience for an endorsed product or service, a Reddit contributor with a high karma score cannot make such a promise. Each post or comment must, in the words of Reddit's co-founder Steve Huffman, "earn its visibility" (Huffman, 2021).

If karma cannot be converted to influence or money, then why do contributors pursue it? Greater visibility and endorsements of one's posts or comments through upvoting is likely to produce feelings of affirmation and connection with (and/or influence over) others, feelings that most people naturally seek out (Barkow, 1975; Gilbert, 1997). As with nearly all online metrics, the system for rewarding karma is subject to manipulation. Contributors may post a 100 versions of the same post, experimenting by posting it with different titles at different times of the week, and then deleting the underachieving versions so as to appear to have a perfect record of popular posting.

If Reddit's design features all have something in common, it is that they de-emphasize the user's individual identity in favor of what they have to say. Individual users have reputations and visible histories, which create some sense of accountability, but these attributes are not foregrounded the way they are on other social media platforms or in many offline contexts. Consequently, each subreddit seems to speak with a disembodied collective voice – from no one in particular to no one in particular. This mode of address is a return to the anonymous, "to-whom-it-may-concern" mode favored in the early days of newsprint (Starr, 2004).

Approaches to understanding Reddit

This chapter provides some basic answers to the question of what Reddit is. Subsequent chapters provide more in-depth answers. They draw from a variety of scholarly disciplines including communication studies, sociology, psychology, and information science, offering insights into the social impact of Reddit, its history, and its place in the history of communication technologies.

In these chapters, I hope to convey some of the breadth and depth of Reddit that heretofore has gone unconsidered. This is not to diminish the importance of existing scholarly research on Reddit, much of which has been an invaluable resource for the writing of this book. The first pass at trying to understand any vast, rapidly changing entity or system inevitably focuses on issues of immediate concern that, if left unaddressed, could result in irreversible damage to individuals or societies. Press coverage and early scholarship on Reddit have addressed such issues comprehensively and articulately, and I invite the interested reader to review these resources (e.g., Lagorio-Chafkin, 2018; Massinari, 2015). Consider this book a second pass at understanding Reddit; something slower and more deliberate.

My inclination to dedicate an entire book to a single platform, and your inclination to read it, implies that there is something special or noteworthy about Reddit. This "platform exceptionalism," common to scholars and technology designers eager to carve out niches in their respective marketplaces, is somewhat artificial. Reddit is not unique in every respect, sharing several important attributes with Twitter and online message boards such as Usenet and 4chan. All are asynchronous, mostly pseudonymous, mostly text, and all facilitate the sharing of content.

Researchers have created useful attribute-based taxonomies for understanding categories of media technologies. Using these frameworks, we can distinguish platforms like Reddit and Twitter from Facebook, which tends to cluster users together based on offline connections rather than interests, and from YouTube and Instagram, which are primarily visual rather than textual. Reddit, Twitter, and many message boards are what Patrick O'Sullivan and Caleb Carr call "masspersonal" technologies (O'Sullivan & Carr, 2018): they facilitate one-to-many communication rather than small-group communication (e.g., GroupMe) or mass communication (e.g., television). It is not surprising, then, to find commonalities between the cultures and social impact of Reddit and those of Twitter. Having said this, there are important differences in attributes – such as the modularity of Reddit – that set Reddit and Twitter apart from one another, while Reddit's massive scale sets it apart from other message boards websites or platforms.

The process that led to the writing of this book involved extensive quantitative analyses of Reddit's evolution coupled with prolonged browsing of Reddit's posts and comments. Some of this browsing was archival: deliberate and systematic, facilitated by navigable databases made freely available to the public.[1] Much of it was leisurely and haphazard, guided by motivations familiar to most Reddit users: a thirst for something entertaining, enlightening, or merely diverting.

The original analyses appearing in this book are chiefly quantitative and descriptive. For the most part, the tools of quantitative analysis are not used in this book to test claims but rather to provide readers with a new vantage point from which to examine the long evolution of Reddit. While such analyses have the virtue of allowing us to see a great deal of human behavior all at once – both in terms of the quantity of behavior and the amount of time covered – they are often subject to a bias toward the easily measured. Page views and unique monthly users are common metrics used to connote popularity or influence online, their commonness allowing for apples-to-apples comparisons across websites and platforms. But these numbers tell us little about user engagement.

This book makes use of a wider variety of metrics – numbers of subreddits, subscribers, contributors, voters, distribution of participation, distribution of votes – in an effort not to rely on a single, limited measure of Reddit's development. Examples of specific subreddits are invoked to illustrate the characters of Reddit's communities and discourse. These methods come with limitations, and my hope is that these limitations are interpreted as an invitation: there is so much more of Reddit to be explored, so many more approaches to understanding how it works.

The bigger picture

Though I aspire to render a big picture of the communities of Reddit, I am not attempting to tell a complete nor perfectly objective story of Reddit. The subreddits I have chosen to examine in detail in subsequent chapters of the book have been chosen mostly to provide the reader with a variety of flavors – different sizes, different sensibilities – rather than as an attempt to provide a perfectly representative sample of all of Reddit. Analysis of such a sample is a larger project – one that is possible given the massive data sets and data analysis tools that are now available.

I approached this project with few specific hypotheses, with more of a desire to engage in some informed speculation as to what Reddit's evolution can teach us about how and why groups change over time. What can we hope to gain by closely examining Reddit, other than a more detailed version of the preceding description? There is a way in which Reddit can be seen as a microcosm of culture online, a perspective of considerable value given the many aspects of our lives that are now partially or fully submerged in the digital world. As communities change and grow, online and offline, an understanding of Reddit may reveal the limits and potential of our lives together.

Note

1 https://files.pushshift.io/reddit/; https://redditsearch.io; https://frontpagemetrics.com/; https://subredditstats.com/

References

Barkow, J. H. (1975). Prestige and culture: A biosocial interpretation. *Current Anthropology, 16*(4), 553–572.

Bruns, A. (2007, June). Produsage: Towards a broader framework for user-led content creation. Paper presented at the Creativity and Cognition 6th conference, Washington, DC, 13–15 June.

Collins, M. P., & Berge, Z. L. (1997, March). Moderating online electronic discussion groups. *American Educational Research Association Conference.*

Gibson, A. (2019). Free speech and safe spaces: How moderation policies shape online discussion spaces. *Social Media + Society, 5*(1), 2056305119832588.

Gilbert, P. (1997). The evolution of social attractiveness and its role in shame, humiliation, guilt and therapy. *British Journal of Medical Psychology, 70*(2), 113–147.

Grimmelmann, J. (2015). The virtues of moderation. *Yale Journal of Law & Technology, 17,* 42–109.

Huffman, S. (2021). Testimony to the United States house of representatives committee on financial services hearing on "Game Stopped? Who Wins and Loses When Short Sellers, Social Media, and Retail Investors Collide." Congress.gov. https://www.congress.gov/117/meeting/house/111207/witnesses/HHRG-117-BA00-Bio-HuffmanS-20210218.pdf

Kriplean, T., Beschastnikh, I., & McDonald, D. W. (2008). Articulations of wikiwork: Uncovering valued work in wikipedia through barnstars. In *Proceedings of the 2008 ACM conference on computer supported cooperative work* (pp. 47–56). ACM: San Diego, CA.

Lagorio-Chafkin, C. (2018). *We are the nerds: The birth and tumultuous life of Reddit, the Internet's culture laboratory.* New York: Hachette Books.

Massanari, A. (2015). *Participatory culture, community, and play: Learning from Reddit.* New York: Peter Lang.

Matias, J. N. (2019) The civic labor of volunteer moderators online. *Social Media + Society, 5*(2), 2056305119836778.

Matias, J. N., Simko, T., & Reddan, M. (2020). Study results: Reducing the silencing role of harassment in online feminism discussions. Citizens and Tech. https://citizensandtech.org/2020/06/reducing-harassment-impacts-in-feminism-online/

Nonnecke, B., & Preece, J. (1999, January) Shedding light on Lurkers in Online Communities. Presented at *Ethnographic studies in real and virtual environments: Inhabited information spaces and connected communities* (pp. 123–128), Edinburgh.

O'Sullivan, P. B., & Carr, C. T. (2018). Masspersonal communication: A model bridging the mass-interpersonal divide. *New Media & Society, 20*(3), 1161–1180.

Preece, J. (2000). *Online communities: Designing usability, supporting sociability.* Chichester: John Wiley & Sons.

Redditinc.com (2021). Reddit. https://www.redditinc.com/advertising/audience

Seering, J., Wang, T., Yoon, J., & Kaufman, G. (2019). Moderator engagement and community development in the age of algorithms. *New Media & Society, 21*(7), 1417–1443.

Starr, P. (2004). *The creation of the media: Political origins of modern communication.* New York: Basic Books.

u/daniel. (2018). Reddit. https://www.reddit.com/r/changelog/comments/9n3ix9/rpopular_is_changing/

u/KeyserSosa. (2010). Reddit. https://www.reddit.com/r/blog/comments/bflwx/just_clearing_up_a_few_misconceptions/

2 The evolutions of Reddit

A disproportionate number of those first to communicate on the internet were futurists. As futurists, they were apt to speculate about the potential of online or "virtual" communities. The engineering feats that led to the development of popular networked communication in the mid-to-late 20th century were undertaken at a time when the speculative science fiction of Isaac Asimov and William Gibson sketched out a rough draft of our networked future. Engineers, scholars, and computer scientists of the day were chiefly concerned with the practical realities of wiring the world together, but could not resist looking into the future. What would it be like when computer-mediated communication became widely available, expanding beyond a small circle of university researchers, when hundreds of millions of people from around the world came together for the first time?

Decades later, we have the luxury of approaching questions posed by futurists from the perspective of an archivist. By paying close attention to how a platform like Reddit grew during its first 15 years – how its contributors, moderators, and administrators continually reshaped its content, discourse, and design – we might come to better understand the platform's relationship with cultures and society. In doing so, we can begin to test the speculations of the futurists who helped form the sociotechnical milieu from which Reddit arose.

Beginnings

In its first stage of development – mid-2005 to early 2006 – Reddit consisted of a single list of posts ranked by popularity, undifferentiated by topic. This first iteration conveyed what was popular among or resonated with the young and tech-savvy, and did it well enough to be considered of value to a small, loyal userbase. This earliest stage was similar to the early stages of most new online communities:

DOI: 10.4324/9781003150800-2

contributions from creators of the communities account for the majority of its content.

Prior to the popularization of the internet, this practice of "seeding" communities was seen as an important step toward achieving sustainability (Preece, 2000). Large groups of users did not yet roam freely across the internet, making it more difficult to quickly amass a userbase capable of supplying the links to novel, appealing content needed to create an appealing destination. Word-of-mouth – that sought-after engine of growth – was just beginning to circulate through blogs, joining established face-to-face social networks and those cultivated through marketing as the means by which ideas travelled. It would take the rise of social platforms like MySpace and Digg, most of which were in their infancy, to create the networked information infrastructure that enabled smaller creations like Reddit to be discovered by the general public. Until then, seeding was seen as necessary to "prime the pump" of ostensibly user-driven communities.

Reddit's first posts linked mostly to traditional news sources such as Reuters, CNN, and *The New York Times*, with some links to smaller, tech-savvy news sites (e.g., CNET, Wired) and, occasionally, blogs. Links to discrete pieces of media content – like a video of Jon Stewart's commencement address at The College of William and Mary, hosted by the college's website – were rare at a time before YouTube, Twitter, and popular image hosting hubs such as Imgur. Several posts recommend and link to other platforms such as Google Video or Pandora, blurring the line between self-expression and endorsement that would, in the coming era of influencers, become nearly invisible. As early as February 2006, Reddit was used by marketers to direct traffic to their websites.[1] Almost immediately, these marketers were criticized by other users, inspiring some of the first conversations[2] on Reddit about the ethics and logistics of deleting posts and banning users. But the majority of posts resembled the lists then populating homepages of other social news sites like Slashdot and Digg: news of interest to a tech-savvy userbase.

Differentiation

By the time Reddit began to differentiate into subreddits in January of 2006, there were roughly 5,000 submissions per month from a few hundred contributors. It's interesting to pause and consider why differentiation occurred at this point. Pornography, like marketing, seems to find its way on to most new communication technologies until regulatory or technological barriers are erected to eliminate or sequester it. The first subreddit – r/nsfw (an abbreviation for "not safe for work" and an acknowledgment that much leisure Reddit browsing occurred at work) – was created to sequester sexually explicit content, but the subreddits that followed were products of another process.

As Reddit became more popular and added users and contributions, the single list of ranked posts grew to a length that made it increasingly unlikely that users would see the majority of the contributions. Original conceptions of the expanding online information marketplace highlighted the benefits of near-infinite "shelf-space." The reduction of barriers to entry would result in exposure to a greater diversity of content, as users sampled less popular options from the far end of the distribution "tail" (Anderson, 2007). The reality of sites on which subsequent visibility is driven by prior selection behavior, like Google and Reddit, is a "rich-get-richer," "winners-take-all" model of audience distribution in which contributions that fail to garner initial attention sink to the bottom and stay there. This so-called "superstar" effect was evident in many offline markets with relatively low barriers to entry and abundant options such as music and publishing (Crain & Tollison, 2002; Marshall, 1890/2013), though online popularity ranking systems made the process – which is as psychological and social as it is technical – more efficient. This often yielded information landscapes as homogenous as those produced in traditional media contexts. Differentiation into subreddits was the first of many administrator interventions designed to push users further down the distribution tail, to help undiscovered content find an audience and thereby diversify exposure.

Of course, differentiation served a more straightforward purpose: making posts related to particular topics easier to find. Reddit had no workable means by which to search or sort posts by topic; topic-specific subreddits provided an elegant solution. Online, precedents existed on popular message boards like Usenet which offered different boards for different topics. Offline, the process of differentiating content or information by topic is so common as to seem an inevitable consequence of growing content universes. To be useful at a certain size, differentiation is necessary.

A typology of subreddits

Subreddits may be divided into types or genres in a number of ways.[3] Not everyone will agree on the usefulness or accuracy of any typology. Acts of classification are frequently occasions for conflict, loaded as they are with aesthetic and moral judgment (Bowker & Star, 2000). But given the number of subreddits (well over 1 million and growing), it is helpful to categorize them in order to understand the breadth of Reddit's communities and to understand how and why Reddit changed over the years.

While categorizing subreddits by topic manages to accurately convey most of its breadth, subreddits became so different in use that "topic" seems an insufficiently inclusive designation. Additionally, some subreddits relate to very specific topics (e.g., r/dating_advice) while others relate only to a content format (e.g., r/pics). For these reasons, the following typology focuses more on *purpose* than on topic. They are categories with blurry edges, not entirely mutually exclusive. One subreddit may exhibit properties of multiple categories, but most subreddits tend toward one of the following uses more than others. The categories are intended to provide, at the very least, a point of orientation for grasping the different uses of Reddit and their evolutions over time.

Spectacle

Posts on these subreddits are typically images or short videos with minimal context provided in the post's title. Like early cinema, the point is to evoke an immediate emotional reaction: awe, adoration, arousal, disgust (Gunning, 1986/2018). The content engages the user on a sensual level, relying less on specific cultural knowledge or context and is therefore more (though not entirely) universal in its appeal. Posts on these subreddits are well suited to a media choice environment that offers abundant options and favors low time commitment and short bursts of attention. Their potency lies in their brevity and immediacy. They are to be looked at rather than discussed, and so these subreddits tend to have a higher subscriber-to-comment ratio than others. Some of these subreddits require that only original content (e.g., photos or video taken by the user) be posted or require that original content be tagged or marked as such, while others permit posting content found elsewhere. Examples include r/video, r/pics, r/aww, r/woahdude, r/oddlysatisfying, r/mildlyinteresting, r/food, r/gonewild, and r/EarthPorn.

Subreddits with posts intended to evoke a sense of moral judgment constitute a sub-type of this category. As with posts in other spectacle subreddits, these posts are typically images or short video that provoke strong visceral reactions (typically of anger or disgust) but there is also an element of moral judgment – anger at seeing bad behavior go unpunished (e.g., r/FuckYouKaren) or satisfaction and righteousness at seeing people receive their comeuppance (e.g., r/instantkarma). In addition to evoking outrage, posts in these subreddits may also provide humor – the subjects depicted in the posts are there to be laughed at. As American politics and culture became more polarized, moral judgments were more frequently linked to political identity. On these subreddits, it is common to find content that has been "poached" from other sources – other platforms such as YouTube, Twitter, or TikTok, or headlines from news websites.

The appeal of moral judgment subreddits has roots in morality plays with most of the narrative elements stripped away, leaving only an implied lesson about good or bad conduct. They also function as a way to "call out" or call public attention to behavior or beliefs deemed to be bad, for the purposes of marshalling public disapproval (i.e., public shaming). Reddit explicitly forbids harassment and other forms of vigilante justice, though this does not guarantee that negative attention accumulated on Reddit will not lead to harassment elsewhere. Most of the depicted behaviors or stated beliefs occur in public or semi-public spaces, and though subjects' faces are often visible, subjects are often treated as an example of a broader social phenomenon. Even when the bad behavior goes unpunished, subscribers to these popular subreddits are able to experience the comfort of solidarity, of knowing that they are not alone in their outrage.

Appreciation, affinity, and fandom (AAF)

Many subreddits focus on media texts (e.g., books, music, movies, video games) or other spectator experiences (e.g., sports). Some of these pertain to general categories (r/movies, r/sports) while others are dedicated to specific genres, texts, sports, teams, or individuals. As the subjects of these subreddits tend to be intellectual property owned by litigious multi-billion-dollar entities, and as Reddit (unlike YouTube) has no mechanism for converting user attention into revenue for the property owners, posts tend to merely refer to texts or performances or include short clips of them. In contrast to spectacle subreddits, AAF subreddits feature a far greater number of comments per post. Posts about live sporting events regularly amass more than 10,000 comments in a few hours, functioning as a kind of archived, searchable live chat.

Communities of fandom were among the first uses of asynchronous online communication technology, the medium serving to facilitate communication among far-flung affinity groups (Baym, 2000; Massanari, 2015). Such technology is also well suited to maintaining running commentaries to texts that unfold over many years. As hubs of affiliation and discourse, AFF subreddits draw fans together in loose congregations, in contrast to fans on Twitter and YouTube that tend to be "atomized" across the platforms. Beyond simply sharing sentiments of appreciation, contributors to these subreddits engage in what Alex Bruns (2007) calls "produsage": debating meanings, cataloging aspects of the texts (Sköld, 2015), offering critiques, authoring alternate versions (i.e., fan fiction and fan art), sharing news, and circulating paratexts (ancillary media objects that extend the pleasure of the frustratingly finite text that is the focus of the fandom; Gray, 2010). Humor – typically in the form of image macro "memes" – is frequently used to praise, critique, or joke about sports and media texts, blurring the boundaries between AAF subreddits and creativity/humor subreddits that are chiefly composed of memes. Memes are often used as a way to inject novelty into discussions of a static text from the past, relating it to current trends in a playful manner. We need look no further than Reddit's thousands of AAF communities to find abundant evidence of the active audiences Henry Jenkins and other fandom scholars have long praised (Jenkins, 2002). Examples include: r/music, r/nba, r/gameofthrones, r/wow.

The public sphere

Many subreddits relate to matters of public or societal concern, a use that corresponds roughly to the concept of the public sphere in sociology and political science (Habermas, 1962/1991). Most of these subreddits relate to current events (e.g., r/news, r/politics), existing primarily to bring attention to and spur discussions about public figures and affairs. The tendency of these subreddits to focus on American public affairs reflects Reddit's origins in the United States. Subreddits like r/worldnews have been created to expand the purview of such discussions. One popular and unique subreddit, r/IAmA, allows contributors to collectively interview public figures, eliminating the barrier between public figure and public discourse.

Public sphere subreddits are similar to AAF subreddits in several ways. Like fandom subreddits, they are descended (and not especially different) from some of the earliest discussion boards on the internet. Subreddits dedicated to particular political parties or figures resemble subreddits dedicated to sports or movie franchises in their strong partisanship and zealous, loyal devotion to objects of adoration. However, discussions relating to politics and current events tend to lack the appreciative language and self-deprecating humor that is common to fandom on Reddit, tending instead toward negativity and seriousness. Comments in these subreddits are somewhat akin to comments on news websites and news commentary on Twitter, and their relationships to democracy and journalism are discussed in subsequent chapters. Posts in non-current-event public sphere subreddits tend to be self-posts rather than links to news articles or other media. Examples include: r/news, r/Conservative, r/Technology.

Personal experience, opinion sharing, and conversation (PEOSC)

Other discussion-oriented subreddits tend to focus less on news headlines or larger, more diffuse societal concerns and more on personal experiences or opinions of Reddit users. The vast majority of posts in these subreddits are self-posts. r/AskReddit is the largest of this type, possessing far more comments per day than any other subreddit. Discourse tends to be supportive or positive (Park & Conway, 2017), though conversations in these subreddits are not immune to strong disagreement and hostility. PEOSC subreddits may be comprised of experiences and opinions relating to particular topics or circumstances (e.g., r/tifu, an abbreviation for "Today I Fucked Up"), or of particular groups of people (e.g., r/teenagers). Examples include r/AskReddit, r/TwoXChromosomes, and r/GetMotivated.

Educational

Some subreddits function as places to exchange information, links to resources, and tips for learning about topics or developing skills in particular domains. Similar to PEOSC subreddits, this type of subreddit exists primarily to exchange support and engage in helpful conversation. Many of these subreddits are "communities of practice" (Wenger, 1998): groups sharing an interest, committed to improving their knowledge and abilities in that domain. Several larger subreddits modeled after r/AskReddit and r/IAmA, such as r/askscience or r/AskHistorians, function primarily as learning communities: opportunities for contributors to ask questions of domain experts, all of whom are required by moderators to cite scholarly sources when answering questions. Posts on one popular general-topic subreddit, r/todayilearned, consist of noteworthy facts learned by the contributor, chiefly from somewhat obscure Wikipedia entries. Examples include r/Python, r/Korean, and r/LanguageLearning.

Creativity

These subreddits exist to showcase the creative work of contributors and, in some cases, discuss the process of creativity. Though posts in these subreddits are similar to spectacle posts that feature original content, the appeal of posts in creativity subreddits are derived primarily from the creative choices made by the contributor, not from the attractiveness or noteworthiness of the depicted subject. Humor subreddits represent a robust sub-type of creativity subreddits. Though some contributors are professional or aspiring artists, many engage in what Jean Burgess (2006) calls "vernacular creativity": something more impermanent, amateur, conversational, and "everyday" than work created to be bought, sold, or enshrined in a museum. Examples include r/photoshopbattles, r/WritingPrompts, and r/dankmemes.

Place-based

Some of the first subreddits were dedicated to particular countries, regions, or cities. They commonly feature posts about news related to those places, and the comments on these posts can resemble those of public sphere subreddits. Place-based subreddits also feature posts about lost pets, apartments for rent, and queries from new residents. Few of these subreddits have become especially popular, perhaps due to the finite number of individuals with ongoing interests in discussions and news relating exclusively to those places, or to competition from other place-based social platforms such as YikYak and Nextdoor, or because the internet, as some scholars predicted (e.g., Castells, 1996), has diminished or altered the relevance of physical places. Examples include r/vancouver, r/de, and r/ASU.

A brief history of Reddit

With the breadth and variety of Reddit's subreddits established, we can begin to examine how they developed over time.[4] Doing so gives us some idea of how Reddit, as a whole, shifted in purpose and character. The following section describes what types of subreddits were created at different stages of Reddit's development as well as the degree to which particular subreddits went on to flourish.

The first wave (2006–2007)

Initially, subreddits could only be created by Reddit administrators, leading them to be created at a relatively slow pace: typically one or two per month, with a surge of 24 subreddits created in February 2006. These subreddits coexisted with a general-purpose, undifferentiated default page – reddit.com – which, until early 2008, accounted for the majority of Reddit's posts. Subreddits from this era can be thought of as emergent niches, the most popular of which are related to politics, science, or technology.

Among the first subreddits to be created, in February 2006, were several place-based subreddits corresponding to different regions (e.g., r/eu for Europe) or countries (e.g., r/ru for Russia). They suggest Reddit's initial global aspirations, but most failed to catch on. In the case of r/it (for Italy), the unsuccessful subreddit was later repurposed as a sparsely populated subreddit dedicated to questions about information technology ("I.T." being a common abbreviation for "information technology"). One of these place-based subreddits, r/de (short for "Deutschland" or Germany), became an active, sustained community (over 400,000 subscribers and 2000 comments per day as of May 2021). The failure of most non-English subreddits is unsurprising given the way the internet was divided by language at the time (Warschauer, 2002).

r/olympics was also created in February 2006 and has survived and thrived in a periodic fashion, dramatically increasing in activity in the lead-up to and during Olympic competitions from 2012 onward. r/olympics serves as a good example of a subreddit that experiences regular, periodic surges in participation and traffic, common among sports and politics subreddits in which surges correspond to competitions or elections held at regular intervals. The most successful of the subreddits founded in early 2006 is r/programming, which has over 3 million subscribers and a few hundred comments per day as of mid-2021. It is the first educational subreddit, existing mostly as a place to share links to resources before including more self-posts intended to generate conversation.

While news had always been part of reddit.com's core content, explicitly political subreddits started in March 2006 with the creation of r/moveon, the first political advocacy subreddit. r/moveon, named for the liberal political action group, failed to gain traction, suggesting that Reddit may have been of limited use as a tool for political action. It wasn't until political advocacy became focused on individual political figures (i.e., "candidate advocacy") that Reddit's potential as a tool for political action became apparent.

In March 2007, the first subreddit dedicated to a political figure – r/obama – was created. It is unclear as to whether someone associated with then-U.S.-presidential-candidate Barack Obama had anything to do with its creation or moderation, or to what extent members of Obama's campaign were aware of it or used it. r/obama goes through several stages of development, blurring the line between niche news and an informal political action group. Initially, posts in r/obama linked to mainstream news outlet's coverage of Obama, some of which was critical or at least skeptical of the candidate. The subreddit went dormant for much of 2007, ramping up activity after Obama's primary victories in early 2008, at which point more posts become more likely to endorse Obama and vilify his rival, Senator Hillary Clinton. Most comment threads and vote counts remain small (typically no more than 100 comments or votes per post). By summer of 2008, activity increased (up to 300 votes and 150 comments). Discussions are often nuanced and civil, including debates about Obama's stance on various issues. By the end of summer 2008, r/obama more closely resembles the kind of candidate advocacy subreddit that became a recurring Reddit motif (e.g., r/Sanders4President, r/

The_Donald, r/MurderedByAOC). By this time, the subreddit featured more self-posts from professed Republicans who were ready to vote for Obama and motivational posts that encourage people to donate to the campaign, and post titles took on the partisan, affect-laden style pioneered by *The Huffington Post*, a popular blog at the time.

r/politics was created in August of 2007, becoming the most active subreddit by the end of 2007. At its start, posts related to news topics of interest to r/politics's largely American constituency (e.g., ongoing conflicts in Iran and Syria; bias against atheist politicians), but most of its popular posts concerned presidential candidate Ron Paul. Many post titles focused on the lack of coverage of Paul's campaign in the mainstream media. This positioning of Reddit as the democratic, authentic alternative to biased, elite traditional news sources presaged the rise of support for Donald Trump eight years later.

In October 2007, a backlash to pro-Ron-Paul posts developed. Many of the most highly upvoted posts are critical of Paul, but the comments on these posts, by and large, defend him. This counter-intuitive dynamic in which the opinion endorsed by the post is contracted by the majority of comments is a reminder that the voting constituency and contributors of a subreddit are not necessarily the same. By March 2008, r/politics's popular posts shifted away from Paul to focus on Obama, though these posts are not so much endorsements of Obama as arguments against his political opponents (e.g., Hillary Clinton, Sarah Palin) or his critics. This highly charged, negative-leaning rhetoric recurs in r/politics during U.S. presidential cycles.

In addition to news and politics, science and video games emerged as topics of flourishing subreddits. r/science, created in October of 2006, was composed mostly of links to traditional news sources' coverage of science news, and occasionally linked to science blogs. As time went on, some popular posts' titles tended toward the sensationalist, and links to humor sites such as Cracked.com were not unheard of. By 2010, it featured more self-posts prompting discussions of specific science topics, as well as more links to original scholarly research articles, though links to coverage of science in the popular press continued to be prevalent.

As r/science grew in popularity, it became more tightly moderated. r/science moderators removed posts with sensationalist titles, attempts at humor, or popular press coverage that did anything more than summarize research findings. Comments containing personal anecdotes or jokes were also removed. As a result, r/science tended to have fewer posts, comments, and contributors than other popular subreddits. By contrast, r/gaming was loosely moderated, perhaps in part because it functioned initially as a locus of fan discourse as much as a place to discuss gaming-related news. Many of r/gaming's most popular posts were self-posts – questions about personal experiences or opinions or anecdotes that inspired other anecdotes. In later years, many posts linked to clips of gaming footage and memes, adding spectacle to ongoing news and fan discourse.

Under Reddit's popular surface, an increasing number of ultimately unsuccessful subreddits were being created. Some, like r/freeculture (advocating free exchange of information online) were indicative of the values of Reddit's creators and early contributors but never grew beyond a few hundred contributors. Subreddits named after many common English-language first names (e.g., r/joel) were created in 2006, and in the absence of any clear purpose, they feature stray posts about programming and little other activity. It is a period of experimentation, a kind of test run which expanded dramatically in January 2008 when Reddit allowed contributors to create their own subreddits.

Flourishing (2008–2009)

On January 25, 2008, 230 new subreddits were created by contributors. These included subreddits for specialized spectacle (r/funny, r/aww for cute content), general categories of fan interest (r/music, r/television), more specific fan interests (r/hiphop, r/The_Wire for the television program *The Wire*), places (r/Boston, r/florida, r/Drexel), emotions or feelings (r/happy, r/Sexy), public sphere discussion (r/news), particular religious and political beliefs (r/Conservative, r/Christianity), conspiracies (r/911truth), websites (r/youtube), and educational domains (r/Economics). Most of what Reddit would eventually become – the variety of its eventual uses – is visible in these subreddits. From this point onward, Reddit's continued differentiation is chiefly further specification of these uses and subreddits corresponding to emerging trends, media texts, or world events.

While several subreddits created on this day would go on to be among its most popular and active, many never took off. It was unclear how broad or specific subreddits should be. While r/funny flourished, r/Animals did not, perhaps because it was unclear as to whether contributors' posts should relate to animal welfare, cute pets, or animals in the news. Following the lead of r/obama, several subreddits for U.S. presidential candidates were created (e.g., r/Romney) though none ultimately flourished.

After this initial explosion, there is a trickle of new subreddits created each day, reaching roughly 40 per day by mid-2008. The minting of new subreddits at this stage resembles a land grab, with some subreddits that are still plainly too vague (e.g., r/radio, r/future), some of which go on to become moderately successful (r/cycling, which has over 200,000 subscribers and a few hundred comments per day, as of mid-2021), and others of which are highly successful specifications of broader existing categories (r/cats).

There is a kind of normative evolution of subreddits observable at this time, whereby subreddits dedicated to broad categories of interest are created first and retain popularity for years to come. Over time, increasingly specific subreddits are created to serve smaller pre-existing niches, affinity groups whose interests were not adequately represented in larger subreddits (often because they were not among Reddit's initial users), or emergent sub-sub-genres that naturally proliferate as cultures evolve. In the realm of AAF subreddits, r/Music (created January 25, 2008 with 27 million subscribers as of mid-2021) is followed by r/classicalmusic (created May 10, 2008 with 1.3 million subscribers as of mid-2021) and other subreddits for pre-existing music genres (r/rap) or new ones (r/Vaporwave). In humor subreddits, r/funny is proceeded by r/memes, which is followed by r/dankmemes and r/deepfriedmemes. There is a saturation point for most categories – the point at which it is subdivided to such a degree that the steady stream of novel, worthwhile content needed to sustain a subreddit cannot be generated.

There are several notable deviations from this norm. Sometimes, subreddits with broader designations (e.g., r/gifs, r/videos) are effectively rendered obsolete by more specific subreddits (e.g., r/interestingasfuck), as is evidenced by the decline in comment activity in the former which corresponds to rises in comments and posts in the latter. Such cases recapitulate the decline of the general-purpose reddit.com page, which, after a gradual decline in activity from 2008 to 2011, was eliminated. This kind of administrator intervention is uncommon but can have significant effects on the size and activity in subreddits, as when default subreddits were eliminated in 2017.

Moderators' actions can affect the trajectory of subreddits as well. Differences between moderators' judgments and those of the constituents of an established subreddit can result in the creation of a "splinter" subreddit. Splinter subreddits address the same topic and are named similarly to the original subreddit, but adopt different sets of rules or encourage different norms for posting and commenting (e.g., r/cringe and r/cringetopia; r/gaming and r/truegaming). These subreddits can co-exist with the originals, syphon disgruntled contributors away from them, or fail to achieve the momentum their creators hoped would sustain them.

Minor events at formative stages of a subreddit's development can have lasting effects. A comparison of r/cute and r/aww, two subreddits created on the same day with the same purpose, provides an instructive example. Within the first week, r/aww has four posts and r/cute has none. Over the next month, posting in r/cute picks up slightly, but increases at a faster rate on r/aww. r/cute never dies out, but its growth stagnates while r/aww's growth continues unabated.

As with biological evolution, timing and serendipity play roles in determining long-term survival. r/fascinating and r/interesting were created long before r/mildlyinteresting and r/interestingasfuck, and, it could be argued, had more intuitive names. But their creation (in 2008) did not coincide with the need for greater specification of subreddits and the dissolution of reddit.com (in 2011). r/mildlyinteresting's creation date (2012) was much more propitious. r/interestingasfuck was created at roughly the same time as r/fascinating and r/interesting, so timing cannot explain its significant advantage. It's slight edge in activity in the years prior to its explosive growth in 2013 might explain its eventual dominance, though it's hard to know whether its success is owed to its name, constituents' norms, moderators' rules, or another factor.

Changing userbase, changing culture (2010–2020)

The successes or failures of subreddits are also influenced by factors external to Reddit's design or function. During the 2010s, the number of Reddit's monthly users increased more than tenfold.[5] It is likely that the values, preferences, and judgments of these new entrants differed from those of existing users. Changes in Reddit's function and userbase take place against the backdrop of changing global cultures. Such shifts are likely responsible for the flourishing of new types of subreddits during this decade.

2010 saw a continuation of a trend that started in 2009: fewer links to news websites and blogs and more self-posts and images (often memes) from imaging hosting websites such as imgur.com (Singer et al., 2014). Some of the most successful subreddits from this era are PEOSC and creativity communities created from 2010 to 2011. Many of the popular PEOSC subreddits are created to share support (e.g., r/GetMotivated, r/LifeProTips). Quirky PEOSC subreddits like r/explainlikeimfive (in which users offer one another simplified explanations of complex phenomena) and r/Showerthoughts (in which users share philosophical or pseudo-philosophical insights) also flourish. Creative communities formed during this time tend toward increasingly specific veins of humor (e.g., r/AdviceAnimals, r/dankmemes) but also include places to showcase and hone creative skills (e.g., r/WritingPrompts). All of these subreddits rely heavily on self-posts and

OC, making this a period of creativity and originality. This is likely a function of how large the Reddit userbase had become: large enough to encompass people collectively capable of generating novel, noteworthy content or commentary on a regular basis.

The popular subreddits created during 2013 and 2014 tend toward moral judgment spectacle, engaging in mean-spirited humor and showcasing people being hurt (e.g., r/Whatcouldgowrong, r/PublicFreakout, r/instantregret). Though their popularity could be explained by changes in Reddit's userbase and voting constituencies, they also owe their existence to the popularization of smartphone cameras and social media that coincided with their creation. Their posts tend to depict behavior captured via smartphone camera or content posted on other social media platforms (e.g., Twitter or YouTube), rapidly circulated through increasingly large, interconnected online social networks. There are still popular "prosocial" subreddits flourishing at this time, but the civic-minded spirit of those subreddits has been joined by ones showcasing "edgier" content.

In the lead-up to the 2016 U.S. presidential election, many social commentators noted a coarsening of public discourse. More aspects of public life became "politicized," and politics was increasingly polarized and vitriolic. The role of Reddit and its users in that process lies beyond the scope of this chapter, though the increasing harshness of discourse is evident in popular subreddits of the time, as is a reaction to it that can be seen in the rapid ascendance of r/Wholesomememes. Created in September 2016, it served as an alternative to humor subreddits that, never having been particularly wholesome to begin with, could not serve as the respite from mean-spiritedness that Reddit users desired at the time.

Conclusion

As the second decade of the 21st century drew to a close, fewer subreddits were able to achieve the kind of larger subscriber counts attained by subreddits created in Reddit's first years of existence. In Figure 2.1, popular subreddits are shown in terms of when they were created (on the X axis), how many subscribers they had as of 2021 (on the Y axis), and how many daily comments they received as of 2021 (the size of the circles that represent each subreddit). Many of the subreddits with the most subscribers and comments in 2021 were created in 2008. One explanation for this is that newer, popular subreddits such as r/wallstreetbets simply haven't been around long enough to accumulate tens of millions of subscribers. Given another few years, they may well catch

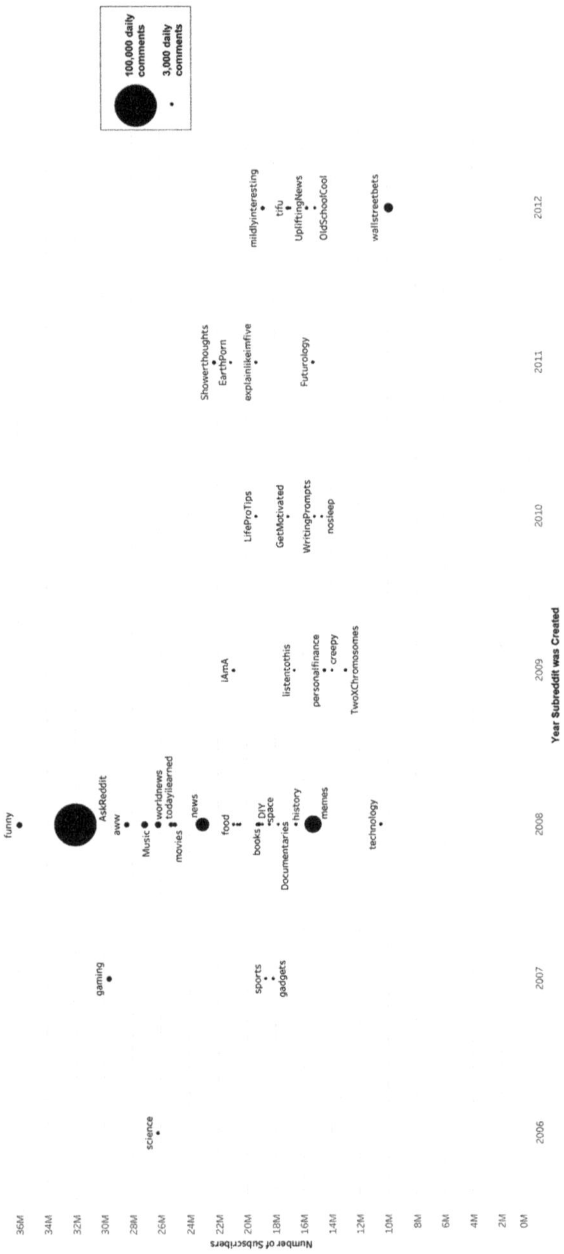

Figure 2.1 Popular Subreddits: Year of creation, subscriber count, and daily comment count.

up to the leaders. Another possibility is that all of the "big tent" inclusive subreddits relating to evergreen topics like politics and movies have already been created, the low-hanging fruit already picked. Contributors seeking to stake their claim encounter the problem of "lateness" commonly faced by innovators who join established spaces.

The seeds of what Reddit would become were visible from the point at which it differentiated into subreddits in early 2008. Despite significant changes to its userbase and the cultures in which its contributors reside, types of subreddits and patterns of user behavior have persisted. This persistence suggests that something about Reddit and its unique structure play a role in shaping users' behavior and the culture of Reddit's communities. Understanding that role requires us to go beyond looking at data and avail ourselves of established theories relating to individuals, technologies, and societies.

Notes

1 https://www.reddit.com/r/reddit.com/comments/170k/alternative_fuel_from_broccoli/
2 https://www.reddit.com/r/reddit.com/comments/1amc/shouldnt_reddit_prevent_this/
3 For examples of other means by which online communities may be classified, see: Brint 2001; Cerulo & Ruane, 1998; Song, 2009.
4 The following synopsis of Reddit's history is based on data from frontpagemetrics.com, subredditstats.com, and redditsearch.io, all of which are publicly available databases tracking the creation and growth of subreddits. See Baumgartner et al., 2020.
5 https://backlinko.com/reddit-users

References

Anderson, C. (2007). *The long tail: How endless choice is creating unlimited demand*. New York: Random House.

Baumgartner, J., Zannettou, S., Keegan, B., Squire, M., & Blackburn, J. (2020, May). The pushshift reddit dataset. In *Proceedings of the international AAAI conference on web and social media* (pp. 830–839). Association for the Advancement of Artificial Intelligence.

Baym, N. K. (2000). *Tune in, log on: Soaps, fandom, and online community*. Thousand Oaks, CA: Sage Publications.

Bowker, G. C., & Star, S. L. (2000). *Sorting things out: Classification and its consequences*. Cambridge, MA: MIT press.

Brint, S. (2001). Gemeinschaft revisited: A critique and reconstruction of the community concept. *Sociological Theory, 19*(1), 1–23.

Bruns, A. (2007, June). Produsage. In *Proceedings of the 6th ACM SIGCHI conference on creativity & cognition* (pp. 99–106). Washington, DC: Association for Computing Machinery.

Burgess, J. (2006). Hearing ordinary voices: Cultural studies, vernacular creativity and digital storytelling. *Continuum*, *20*(2), 201–214.

Castells, M. (1996). *The rise of the network society*. Chichester: John Wiley & Sons.

Cerulo, K. A., & Ruane, J. M. (1998). Coming together: New taxonomies for the analysis of social relations. *Sociological Inquiry*, *68*(3), 398–425.

Crain, W., & Tollison, R. (2002). Consumer choice and the popular music industry: A test of the superstar theory. *Empirica*, *29*, 1–9.

Gray, J. (2010). *Show sold separately: Promos, spoilers, and other media paratexts*. New York: New York University Press.

Gunning, T. (1986/2018). The cinema of attraction[s]: Early film, its spectator and the avant-garde. In N. Dobson, A. H. Roe, A. Ratelle, & C. Ruddell (Eds.) *The animation studies reader* (17–27). New York: Bloomsbury Academic.

Habermas, J. (1962/1991). *The structural transformation of the public sphere: An inquiry into a category of bourgeois society*. Cambridge, MA: MIT press.

Jenkins, H. (2002). Interactive audiences? The collective intelligence of media fans. In D. Harries (Ed.) *The new media book* (pp. 157–170). London: British Film Institute.

Marshall, A. (1890/2013). *Principles of economics. Palgrave classics in economics* (8th ed.). London: Palgrave Macmillan.

Massanari, A. (2015). *Participatory culture, community, and play: Learning from Reddit*. New York: Peter Lang.

Park, A., & Conway, M. (2017). Longitudinal changes in psychological states in online health community members: Understanding the long-term effects of participating in an online depression community. *Journal of Medical Internet Research*, *19*(3), e71.

Preece, J. (2000). *Online communities: Designing usability, supporting sociability*. Chichester: John Wiley & Sons.

Singer, P., Flöck, F., Meinhart, C., Zeitfogel, E., & Strohmaier, M. (2014, April). Evolution of reddit: From the front page of the internet to a self-referential community?. In *Proceedings of the 23rd international conference on world wide web* (pp. 517–522). Seoul: Association for Computing Machinery.

Sköld, O. (2015). Documenting virtual world cultures: Memory-making and documentary practices in the City of Heroes community. *Journal of Documentation*, *71*(20), 294–316.

Song, F. W. (2009). *Virtual communities: Bowling alone, online together*. New York: Peter Lang.

Warschauer, M. (2002). The internet and linguistic pluralism. In I. Snyder (Ed.) *Silicon literacies: Communication, innovation and education in the electronic age* (pp. 62–74). London: Routledge.

Wenger, E. (1998). Communities of practice: Learning as a social system. *Systems Thinker*, *9*(5), 2–3.

3 Reddit in context

"For a while after the episode ended, my mind was pretty much a blank. That surprised me, since I'd expected to like it right away, and I tried to tell myself that I should. But, eventually, it dawned on me: I *didn't* like it. It took me a while to figure this out, too, but there was a group of us who gathered and hotly discussed this episode for a good 2 1/2 hours after it ended, and all of us had separately arrived at the conclusion that none of us were happy with it."[1]

> "...The plotting doesn't make sense anymore. Things don't happen for a *reason*, they happen *just because*. Like a child making up a story with no logical flow, jumping from one cool thing to the next. As though they are going into the writing room with the question 'wouldn't it be cool if...' when they should be asking 'wouldn't it make sense if....'"[2]

One of these comment excerpts was posted in 1993 to an internet forum dedicated to discussions of television shows. The other excerpt was posted 24 years later to a subreddit dedicated to the discussion of a particular television show and book series. These examples of online discourse have been cherry-picked to make a point: much of what we see on Reddit is not unprecedented; it could be seen elsewhere on the internet 20 or even 30 years before the platform was created. As much as the internet and societies have changed over time, some elements of early online life remain relatively unchanged.

Usenet – the collection of internet forums created in the early 1980s from which the first quote is drawn – was similar to Reddit not only in its content but also in terms of its structure and how its users behaved. Just as on Reddit, a small, core group of Usenet contributors produced the vast majority of its content. Like most posts and comments on Reddit, most posts on Usenet did not receive replies. Most

DOI: 10.4324/9781003150800-3

newsgroups (Usenet's equivalent of subreddits) had very little activity while a handful accounted for the bulk of discourse on the forums (Smith, 1999). Early Usenet contributors even wrestled with some fundamental dilemmas about free speech, democracy, and community moderation that would be familiar to any of Reddit's administrators (Hauben & Hauben, 1997, p. 180).

And yet Usenet and Reddit are not precisely the same. Had I selected a comment excerpt at random instead of cherry-picking, differences in topics, etiquette, and speech would have made it obvious as to which excerpt was from the 1990s internet and which was from Reddit in the 2010s. Usenet and Reddit are also different in terms of their social outcomes. Few people would claim that Usenet disrupted societies or industries the way that Reddit is believed by many to have done. Was the difference in outcomes due to a difference in timing (Reddit becoming popular just as the internet was becoming widely accessible), of design (e.g., the ability to upvote and downvote), or something else?

While research on Reddit increased as the platform grew in popularity (Proferes et al., 2021), much of the research focuses on user behavior and ignores the larger cultural, industrial, and historical contexts in which Reddit is embedded. Viewing technologies as socially constructed objects helps us to understand why they are the way they are, and how designers, cultures, and users all influence technologies as they iterate (Bijker, 2008). By considering what the internet was like at the time Reddit came into being, we might gain a better understanding of the cultural forces that shaped its early history. Technologies do not arise fully formed, *ex nihilo*. They are created and re-created by individuals who, implicitly and explicitly, enact their values in their design and use choices.

In this chapter, I examine Reddit's lineage, locating it in a larger history of the popularized internet and describing the cultures and intellectual traditions that informed the creation and modification of these technologies.

Ancestors

The internet is, fundamentally, a network – a tool for joining individuals together like the railway or highway systems of the 19th and 20th centuries. Networks can be used for "top-down" distribution of professionally produced goods or content, customized for and sent directly to individuals. Early iterations of the consumer networked communication technologies, such as the videotex and teletext systems used in 1970s and 1980s Western Europe, were essentially interactive newspapers, allowing users to customize content but not to contribute to it. The long history of interactive television – an innovation that never quite caught on – is a glimpse of what the internet might have been: a tool for customized content dissemination.

Networked communication could also be used for "point-to-point" or interpersonal communication. Email and instant messaging or "chat" programs had been in use at universities since the 1960s, where computer-mediated communication was pioneered. Email and chat programs were faster, cheaper versions of postal mail or long-distance phone calls, both of which were thought of by citizens as means by which to communicate with members of their existing offline social network.

Arguably the most innovative use offered by networked communication technology was its ability to remotely link individuals to one another not in dyads but in groups, the first workable,[3] scalable many-to-many communication technology. This use was envisioned as early as 1968 by psychologist/computer scientist J. C. R. Licklider. In the 1970s, academic researchers developed online forums to facilitate collaboration across great distances. Usenet and bulletin board services (BBSs) hosted discussions among far-flung strangers on a range of topics. In the 1980s, multiplayer video games, in particular, multiplayer online role playing games (MORPGs), served a demand for multiplayer games cultivated by table-top role playing games like *Dungeons and Dragons* and the popular video arcade games of the 1970s.

And yet as the World Wide Web popularized network communication technology in the 1990s, none of these many-to-many uses grew at the speed that top-down and interpersonal uses did. One cause of this discrepancy had to do with a lack of demand. The appeal of text-based user-generated content (UGC) was not obvious in an era when an expanding cable television universe promised to serve niche interests with professionally produced video. Another cause had to do with infrastructure. Corporate content producers had access to content distribution networks that allowed for seamless transmission of data, something that the average user did not have access to (Jamieson, 2016; Sandvig, 2015). These forces kept online communities in a prolonged stasis, largely out of the general public's view.

In addition to Usenet's online groups, there was the WELL (Whole Earth 'Lectronic Link), a virtual community founded in 1985 and extensively chronicled in the writings of Howard Rheingold (1993). Whereas Usenet's primary antecedent was the bulletin board, the WELL modeled itself after Parisian salons of the 17th and 18th centuries. Topics were debated, an etiquette evolved, and social support was exchanged on the WELL. In a precursor to several subreddits such as r/covid19, scientists would submit electronic pre-printed reports of their research for others to peruse and critique. Rheingold draws a distinction between the WELL and "the usual BBS stuff" (p. 38), attributing the distinction to differences between the creators of the two platforms. The WELL was created by counterculture oracle Stewart Brand. Brand hand-picked community hosts, establishing the WELL's default culture – liberal, forward-looking, open-minded.

In *From Counterculture to Cyberculture* (2006), communication scholar Fred Turner describes early virtual communities such as the WELL as the intellectual descendants of utopian counterculture and communes of the 1960s, imbued with some of their spirit and values. These values included a kind of cultural permissiveness as well as a distrust or outright hostility toward authority and capitalism. Though most members of this counterculture expressed a reverence toward nature, this was not necessarily coupled with cynicism toward technology. The willingness to experiment with technology was part of a more general experimental ethos: all ideas and assumptions – about consciousness, family, government, and society itself – required revisiting.

Another philosophy informing the values of early virtual communities can be found in arguments set forth by 18th- and 19th-century political philosophers like John Stuart Mill and Thomas Paine. These philosophers espoused the virtues of democracy and liberalism at a time when neither was widespread. Internet evangelists saw themselves as an extension of this tradition (Hauben & Hauben, 1997). Instead of rebelling against the repressive rule of monarchies and theocracies, virtual community pioneers cast global mega-corporations in the role of the tyrannical power from which the internet – bringer of direct democracy, voice for the voiceless – would deliver us.

Usenet grew out of a system designed by computer scientists to circulate newsletters. By the 1980s, computer programming had developed its own subculture. Hacker culture, as it came to be known, is a culture of poking and prodding, born of a sense of playfulness and mischief (Thomas, 2002). A certain anti-establishment ethos links the utopian counterculture of the 1960s to the hacker culture of the late 20th century; specifically, an opposition to corporate commercialism and its influence on culture. Both possess a sense of apartness from mainstream culture, but hacker culture, in most of its online manifestations, is not as grandiose nor as optimistic as 1960s utopian counterculture. While members of the 1960s counterculture were interested in pushing beyond the limits of consciousness and the human mind, hacker culture was preoccupied with pushing beyond the limits of present technology (Levy, 1984).

Both Usenet and the WELL were small and homogeneous in comparison to the groups that populate Reddit, Twitter, and other popular social platforms of the 21st century. They were comprised not of casual internet users, but rather tech-savvy individuals who were excited by the novelty of forming bonds with strangers. At this stage of development of virtual communities, repeated contact among users was highly likely. Most online forums were like small towns in which people ran into one another and were likely to have certain things in common (e.g., interests, language, socio-economic status). Behavior within these groups, particularly behavior on the WELL, had the building blocks of community: trust, disclosure, and social cohesion. Once you adjusted to the idea that community *could* be established across distance through technology (a claim that early internet scholars spent a great deal of time asserting and re-asserting), it seemed natural to conceive of the relatively small groups that formed online as communities.

The other precursors to Reddit were online lists collectively curated through the process of collaborative filtering. Prior to the advent of networked computing, the business of information curation – the pooling and organizing of knowledge – was chiefly the domain of professional archivists, librarians, and academics. Databases, reference works (e.g., encyclopedias), and catalogs were the results of their labors. The process of "collaborative filtering" effectively harnessed the power of the network to crowdsource the tasks of cataloging and ordering information. The *Internet Movie DataBase* (IMDB) grew out of a Usenet newsgroup discussion thread that sought to catalogue the names of attractive actresses (Weible, 2001). Later, IMDB allowed users to rate movies and television shows on a scale of one to ten. Online customer rating systems like *Angie's List* and *Epinions.com* were modeled after consumer advocacy services (e.g., *Consumer Reports),* allowing users to review products and services for the benefit of other users. More proximate to Reddit, the website *Slashdot* permitted users to submit links to external websites and permitted a select group of users to assign links a value of +1 (for links that were insightful or interesting) or –1 (for links that were redundant or inflammatory) (Johnson, 2002).

Web 2.0

All of these websites were clear antecedents to Reddit and other popular social platforms of the early 21st century, but none were as widely used or contributed to as their descendants. It was not until the broader adoption of online content creation tools in the first years of the 21st century, a phenomenon commonly referred to as "Web 2.0," that mass participation and contribution became possible. Blogs were a text-based, easily updated content creation tool that used little bandwidth and provided readers with a steady stream of novel content. They were chiefly used as a means of identity construction and expression (Gurak & Antonijevic, 2008), something more like a diary and less like a conversation. This drew different types of users into the online participatory universe: less tech savvy, more introspective, more diverse (Lenhart & Fox, 2006). Blogs began to link to one another, forming nascent online social networks known, collectively, as the blogosphere.

At the same time, a class of websites designed primarily to establish connections among individuals – social networking sites (SNS) – became more popular. Like blogs, SNS were a means of constructing and projecting oneself into a digital space, as well as a way to connect with others (Baym, 2015; boyd, 2010; Turkle, 1995). SNS quickly became the most popular leisure use of the internet, increasing demand for networked communication technology. A smaller, more specialized online culture developed around social bookmarking sites like *del.icio.us,* which grew out of blogs that assembled lists of links to other sites (i.e., linkrolls). *Digg,* Reddit's immediate predecessor, expanded and democratized *Slashdot's* model of user-contributed links voted and commented on by other users. The popularity of these sites quickly increased with the rising number of users who contributed content to the internet. Thirty-five years after J. C. R. Licklider envisioned the possibilities of a many-to-many communication technology, its mass adoption was coming to pass.

How would this influx of new contributors affect sites like Digg and Reddit? Both platforms were more than just conversations; they were places to distribute, find, and consume collaboratively filtered content. As such, they would be affected by growth in fundamentally different ways than sites like the WELL and Usenet. Conversations among large numbers of interlocutors tended to become chaotic or fragmented, breaking into smaller and smaller homogeneous enclaves. Conversely, additional contributions to websites composed of user-generated or user-curated content were thought to have largely positive effects (Benkler, 2008). They allowed these sites to maintain a steady flow of novel content, staving off stagnation. Additional contributors also changed the content of the sites to something that reflected the experiences and preferences of a broader, more heterogeneous public.

What would platforms like Digg and Reddit have been like had they stayed small? Consider the fate of several UGC websites that arose around the same time and from a similar hacker/mischief culture as that which yielded Reddit: *4chan*, *SomethingAwful*, and *YTMND*. All three websites lasted for decades without achieving the kind of mainstream adoption achieved by Reddit. Their contributing userbases were large enough to sustain flows of novel content, but they possessed an insularity of culture, reflecting an unchanging comedic sensibility and worldview. All three struggled to remain financially solvent and lacked the resources needed to add new features that new users came to expect. Even Usenet, one of Reddit's distant ancestors, persists 40 years after its creation, though it is not directly accessible from the World Wide Web.

Reddit culture

Hacker culture was certainly one part of Reddit's original value system. As the internet flourished, governments and corporations sought to control or regulate it in various ways. Hacker culture stood in opposition to this, insisting that information, like speech, should be free. This kind of "free speech fundamentalism" permeates the writings of Reddit co-founder and prolific blogger Aaron Swartz (Swartz, 2015) and was evident in Reddit users' activism against internet regulatory legislation in 2011 and 2012. Swartz, like other successful website designers of the time (e.g., Jimmy Wales and Larry Sanger of *Wikipedia*), was as much a philosopher as he was a computer programmer. His view assumed that choices made by technology designers had broad socio-political implications, and that a certain amount of political activism was necessary in order to defend the virtue of the internet.

One quality that set Reddit apart from many of the aforementioned hacker-centric websites was its connection to entrepreneurial culture of the early 2000s. The first dot-com boom at the turn of the millennium provided the sense that tech-obsessed "nerds" were not necessarily marginal to either the culture or the economy, but rather could be at the forefront of both. The rapid rise of peer-to-peer file-sharing software (e.g., *Napster*) and the success of blogs and early SNSs provided evidence that demand for technology would be driven by social platforms. Business-minded computer programmers and investors turned their attention to this space, though the precise contours of the social web were as yet undefined. The idea for Reddit originated in a meeting between its co-founders, Alexis Ohanion and Steve Huffman, and a venture capitalist, Paul Graham (Lagorio-Chafkin, 2018).

It took shape during the co-founders' time at *Y Combinator*, a tech start-up accelerator.

One immutable imperative of entrepreneurial culture is growth: the need to grow, quickly, at all costs. By the time Reddit was created, popular Web 2.0 websites like Blogger and MySpace had been sold to larger companies, establishing a template for tech investors and entrepreneurs in the emerging information technology economy. As long as websites could amass enough users in a short enough span of time, they could generate significant returns on initial investments, even in the absence of a plan to generate revenue from those users.

This approach to creating and sustaining online communities yielded several high-profile failures. MySpace, the most popular SNS prior to the ascendance of Facebook, suffered a significant decline in users from 2008 to 2011. Sold by News Corporation for a fraction of its purchase price, MySpace's decline sent a message to potential investors about the volatility of the social media market. Digg suffered a much quicker demise. After a controversial re-design, traffic to Digg declined roughly 30% within a month (Wilhelm, 2010). The lessons from these cautionary tales were myriad: dominance in social media markets is more fragile than in other markets; beware meddlesome, acquisitive mega-corporations; avoid radical re-designs or any other sudden movements that might scare off loyal users. Perhaps in response to these lessons, Reddit's design remained largely unchanged for a decade, its founders and investors content to grow at a more gradual rate than other social platforms of the era.

In the public statements from designers of dynamic social environments like Reddit, there is a kind of valorization of organic, unplanned evolution, an attempt to efface the power that they have as designers. Taking such a stance aligns their technology with something that is often considered to be inherently good and pure – organic nature – and sets it apart from that which is inherently fraught and corrupt – market-driven social engineering. Conveniently, it also conveys a sense of modesty and absolves designers of blame if things go poorly. They are not the visionary geniuses who build new objects, but rather benign facilitators. Critical media scholars, then, are in the position of having to unmask designers' roles in the ongoing design process, highlighting the ways in which they have more control over the process than they purport.

How we look at the internet

The cultural perspectives that informed the creation of online communities were often adopted by those who studied it. Foundational scholarly work on the topic of online communities drew from two intellectual wellsprings: speculative works – including the more adventurous writing of Marshall McLuhan (McLuhan & Fiore, 1968) and William Gibson's science fiction – and auto-ethnographies of relatively small-scale group interaction online (Wellman, 2011). Whether celebrating the internet's potential to distribute social capital or lamenting the encroachment of commercial interests in an emerging public sphere, the sentiment was the same: give the people their voice and good things will come. "The Will of the People" was an unquestioned, uncomplicated good.

There is little consideration of how this Will might be manipulated and co-opted, how attempts to measure it would affect what it ultimately conveys, and whether there could be a case in which it would yield a bad outcome. In all the debate about whether virtual communities were real communities, there is little mention of polarization, a topic which comes to dominate questions about the qualities of online discourse 20 years after the internet's popularization. Perhaps, to the Netizens of the 1990s, the idea that enough people would actually rely on online communities as a primary source of information about current events seemed too far fetched.

In her book *Virtual Communities: Bowling Along, Online Together*, Felicia Wu Song (2009) situates much the thinking that animated enthusiasm for virtual communities in the context of Robert Putnam's influential work on social anomie at the end of the 20th century. Putnam notes markers of the breakdown of social bonds of community in Western countries, particularly the United States, and places most of the blame on the ascendance of television (Putnam, 2000). Whether or not television was truly to blame or whether the internet could ameliorate this harm is irrelevant to Song's core argument about the ways in which offline social contexts shaped perceptions of the first online communities: "community" had been defined, and was valued, mostly because it was seen to be in decline.

Many of the groups that formed online after the rise of Web 2.0 bear little resemblance to the groups studied by early internet scholars. The size, scale, and diversity of massive online communities has changed how they function: how likely members of the group are to come into repeated contact with one another; how likely they are to contribute to discussions; how likely they are to share a set of values. Features like the ability to upvote or downvote individual comments also change the social dynamics of online communities: acting as a scalable crowdsourcing of the tasks of managing spam and disruptive behavior while introducing problems of ideological homogeneity and groupthink.

Just as metropolises like New York City are not just larger versions of villages, massive online communities are fundamentally different from the virtual communities that served as the basis for scholarly understanding of the phenomenon.

From a design perspective, we might think of the comments on Reddit as the equivalent of a "living fossil" like a horseshoe crab: an organism that has not changed very much in response to a radically reconfigured environment. While other descendants of the earliest forms of computer-mediated communication developed traits such as networked structures and video, the comments of Reddit remain similar to the asynchronous conversations held in the 1980s and 1990s on BBSs, Usenet, and the WELL. But the values and spirit of Reddit's communities *have* evolved, not by design but rather in response to the influx of users from outside the tech-centric subculture of the platform's origin. If Reddit has a dominant culture, it exists at the intersection of utopian, hacker, personal blogging, and entrepreneurial cultures – a uniquely early 21st-century mix of values.

Notes

1 Posted on Usenet. https://www.usenetarchives.com/view.php?id=rec.arts.tv&mid=PDE5OTNNYXk2LjIwMDA0NS4xMDQ4OUBtaWR3YXkudWNoaWNhZ28uZWR1Pg
2 Posted on Reddit. https://www.reddit.com/r/asoiaf/comments/6quk4r/spoilers_extended_missing_the_point_and_rewarding/dl0skaa/?utm_source=reddit&utm_medium=web2x&context=3
3 Amateur radio preceded networked computing technology by several decades and this technology could be used by an individual to reach many others (one-to-many). Unfortunately, the finite nature of radio bandwidth prevented its widespread use.

References

Baym, N. K. (2015). *Personal connections in the digital age*. Cambridge, MA: Polity Press.

Benkler, Y. (2008). *The wealth of networks*. New Haven, CT: Yale University Press.

Bijker, W. E. (2008). Technology, social construction of. In W. Donsbach, J. Bryant, & R. T. Craig (Eds.) *The International Encyclopedia of Communication*. Chichester: John Wiley & Sons.

boyd, D. (2010). Social network sites as networked publics: Affordances, dynamics, and implications. In Z. Papacharissi (Ed.) *A networked self: Identity, community, and culture on social network sites* (pp. 47–66). New York: Routledge.

Gurak, L. J., & Antonijevic, S. (2008). The psychology of blogging: You, me, and everyone in between. *American Behavioral Scientist, 52*(1), 60–68.
Hauben, M., & Hauben, R. (1997). *Netizens: On the history and impact of Usenet and the Internet.* Piscataway, NJ: IEEE Computer Society Press.
Jamieson, J. (2016). Many (to platform) to many: Web 2.0 application infrastructures. *First Monday, 21*(6).
Johnson, S. (2002). *Emergence: The connected lives of ants, brains, cities, and software.* New York: Simon and Schuster.
Lagorio-Chafkin, C. (2018). *We are the nerds: The birth and tumultuous life of Reddit, the Internet's culture laboratory.* New York: Hachette Books.
Lenhart, A., & Fox, S. (2006). Bloggers: A portrait of the internet's new storytellers. Pew Internet & American Life Project. Pew Research. https://www.pewtrusts.org/-/media/legacy/uploadedfiles/wwwpewtrustsorg/reports/society_and_the_internet/pipbloggers071906pdf.pdf
Levy, S. (1984). *Hackers: Heroes of the computer revolution.* Garden City, NY: Anchor Press/Doubleday.
Licklider, J. C. (1968). The computer as a communication device. *Science and Technology, 76*(2), 21–38.
McLuhan, M., & Fiore, Q. (1968). *War and peace in the global village.* Bantam, NY: Ginko Press.
Proferes, N., Jones, N., Gilbert, S., Fiesler, C., & Zimmer, M. (2021). Studying Reddit: A systematic overview of disciplines, approaches, methods, and ethics. *Social Media + Society, 7*(2), 20563051211019004.
Putnam, R. D. (2000). *Bowling alone: The collapse and revival of the American community.* New York: Simon & Schuster.
Rheingold, H. (1993). *The virtual community: Homesteading on the electronic frontier.* Reading, MA: Addison-Wesley Publishing.
Sandvig, C. (2015). The Internet as the anti-television: Distribution infrastructure as culture and power. In L. Parks and N. Starosielski (Eds.) *Signal traffic: Critical studies of media infrastructures* (pp. 225–245). Urbana: University of Illinois Press.
Smith, M. A. (1999). Invisible crowds in cyberspace: Mapping the social structure of the Usenet. In M. A. Smith & P. Kolluck (Eds.) *Communities in cyberspace* (pp. 195–219). London: Routledge.
Song, F. W. (2009). *Virtual communities: Bowling alone, online together.* New York: Peter Lang.
Swartz, A. (2015). *The boy who could change the world: The writings of Aaron Swartz.* New York: The New Press.
Thomas, D. (2002). *Hacker culture.* Minneapolis: University of Minnesota Press.
Turkle, S. (1995). *Life on the screen.* New York: Simon & Schuster.
Turner, F. (2006). *From counterculture to cyberculture: Stewart Brand, the Whole Earth network, and the rise of digital utopianism.* Chicago, IL: The University of Chicago Press.

Weible, C. L. (2001). The internet movie database: A reference guide to hollywood and beyond. *Internet Reference Services Quarterly*, *6*(2), 47–50.
Wellman, B. (2011). Studying the internet through the ages. In C. Ess & M. Consalvo (Eds.) *The handbook of internet studies* (pp. 17–23). Oxford: Wiley-Blackwell.
Wilhelm, A. (2010). Digg's traffic is collapsing at home and abroad. *The Next Web.* https://thenextweb.com/news/diggs-traffic-is-collapsing-at-home-and-abroad

4 Identity on Reddit

r/BlackPeopleTwitter, as the name suggests, is a subreddit in which contributors post screenshots of Tweets from Black Twitter users. "Black Twitter" has been a locus of cultural performance, humor, and civic activism for Black internet users since the early days of Twitter (Brock, 2012), and most of the content sharing in r/BlackPeopleTwitter is done as a way of showcasing Tweets that contributors find especially funny, important, or true. Comments on r/BlackPeopleTwitter posts tend to reflect this positive orientation toward the tweets, elaborating or riffing on them the way a group of friends might joke *along with* another friend rather than *about* that friend. Whether or not the individuals who participate in these communicative acts – those who post or comment on r/BlackPeopleTwitter, those who vote on posts or comments, those who merely read and enjoy them, and even the Twitter users who post the content in the first place – identify as Black is often unclear.

The ability of internet users to slough off their offline identities and adopt any persona they wish has always been seen as central to the revolutionary potential of computer-mediated communication. The quality of online identity that allows for this relatively easy severing of one's online identity from markers of one's offline identity (e.g., legal name, face) is really a collection of qualities, including increased *malleability* (how easy or difficult it is to change one's identity, as well as the range of options or resources a user possesses when presenting one's self) and decreased *verifiability* (how easy or difficult it is for other users to determine the relationship between a user's online persona and unique markers of their offline identity). Despite its multifaceted nature, this quality has come to be known in popular discourse by a single term: *anonymity*.

Anonymity, in this broad sense, exists in offline contexts as well. Markers of one's identity are often obscured, de-emphasized, or

DOI: 10.4324/9781003150800-4

rendered uninterpretable depending on one's social context. Walking around a city to which you have never been can make you feel "anonymous." The explosion in online anonymity sent communication and internet scholars back to the work of philosophers, sociologists, and psychologists who already understood each individual person to possess multiple, fungible identities that were revealed or concealed in various social contexts (Goffman, 1959; Haraway, 1991; Ryan & Deci, 2012). Twenty years after the popularization of the internet, questions and concerns about online identity continue to focus on its multilayered, fungible qualities.

Such qualities are not only of interest to scholars; members of online communities often debate their merits, alternately celebrating and bemoaning the vagueness and instability of identities online. So it was that these qualities of online identity came to be a topic of discussion among moderators and contributors to r/BlackPeopleTwitter. Within several months of its creation in late 2014, r/BlackPeopleTwitter became one of the fastest-growing subreddits on the site. With the rapid influx of new contributors came questions about the changing character of the community. Given that race is central to the purpose of the subreddit, questions about community character and representation in discourse tended to relate to racial identities. However, other popular subreddits marked as spaces for or about particular identities (e.g., female-identifying; lesbian, gay, bisexual, and transgender) faced similar questions. Given the widespread expectation of anonymity online, can places intended to be by, for, or about one group of people maintain this kind of homogeneous collective identity while growing in the rapid, uncontrolled way that is common among successful online communities? What accounts for the persistent importance of identities grounded in corporeal, offline life in online contexts? And, returning to the purpose of this book, how does the unique mix of attributes possessed by Reddit affect presentations and perceptions of identities?

Presenting and perceiving the self on Reddit

Identity has been defined in many different ways by many scholars in many fields, a full review of which lies beyond the scope of this book. Before proceeding, I briefly describe how identity will be conceptualized in this chapter.

Identity can be treated as an idea: how people conceive of themselves or how they define their selves either in terms of their uniqueness or in terms of their belonging to certain groups and not to others (Seargeant & Tagg, 2014). This idea can be expressed or presented in observable ways: through appearance, speech, or behavior. Though it may be tempting to think of self-presentation as the result of self-conception, self-presentation may influence self-conception, as when a person adopts a new persona and, over time, comes to think of themselves differently as a result of their changed appearance, speech, or behavior. And so, unobservable thought and observable behavior continually influence one another, generating and regenerating identity (Butler, 1988). As this book's methodological approach addresses observable characteristics of Reddit, I turn now to the observable manifestations of identity on the platform.

A natural starting point for thinking about identity on Reddit is the username. For most of the platform's first 15 years,[1] usernames have been the most prominent markers of users' unique identities. Users can choose any name for themselves as long as no other user has already chosen to use it. A user's choice of name may communicate something about them: a certain seriousness or lack thereof; a level of education or cultural literacy; a sense of humor; a particular interest or passion. Some users chose to use their legal names or some variation of them so as to associate their Reddit identities with offline identities,[2] though this is not the norm. Usernames appear above posts and comments in a smaller, gray font.

When a user clicks on another user's name, they are taken to a profile page displaying that user's comments and posts, their karma score, and the age of their account. Looking through a user's previous comments and posts can give you a general sense of who they are – their interests, beliefs, and styles of self-expression – certainly more than what could be gleaned by reading a single post or comment. Someone who may have initially appeared to be nice in one comment may have a history of posting hostile comments, or someone who appeared to be above pop culture at first may be revealed to be a fan of reality television. Even if a user has few or no previous comments or posts, their profile page will display the number of years the account has been active. As in other social contexts, the absence of an observable reputation, or an especially inconsistent history, is often regarded as an evasion of accountability or a sign of inauthenticity. Because Reddit attaches usernames to posting and commenting history, it is often referred to as a *pseudonymous*, rather than anonymous, space.

Comments and posts on profile pages, like comments under any post, can be sorted chronologically or by vote score. These two ways of presenting users' contributions are apt to convey very different impressions. While chronologically sorted contributions provide a "slice of life" occurring at a particular point in time, a user's top-scoring comments and posts portray an idealized self, someone wittier, more interesting, and more appealing than the chronologically sorted self. Significantly, Reddit sorts contributions on profile pages chronologically by default, making it harder for users to present a "curated self" to other users than is the case on most other popular social media platforms.

A user's karma score – the sum of the vote scores of all their comments and posts – gives others a quick sense of how much the user contributes, as higher karma scores can only be achieved by posting or commenting with relative frequency. Beyond that, it expresses the extent to which a user's contributions resonated with other voting Reddit users. One cannot use it to ascribe any particular belief or value to the user; upvotes contributing to this total could have come from a comment extolling the virtues of capitalism posted in a capitalist-friendly subreddit just as easily as they could have come from a comment criticizing capitalism posted in an anti-capitalism subreddit. All upvotes, regardless of how they are acquired, count equally. Interpretations of karma scores – whether they are seen as markers of authority, expertise, or merely experience – likely vary among users.

Some users have labels that appear next to their usernames when they post or comment in certain subreddits. These labels, known as "flair," are recognizable markers not of discrete identity, but of affiliation. In some subreddits, flair confers expertise, as when a professional in a particular field has flair that communicates that status (e.g., medical doctor), while in other cases, it conveys a preference or passion, as with team flairs for fans in sports subreddits. In some cases, flair is chosen by users while in others it is assigned by moderators. The commonness of flair varies among subreddits; most large, popular, general purpose subreddits do not use flair, while in smaller subreddits relating to expertise or fandom they are the norm.

Users are not discouraged from having multiple Reddit accounts, and the practice of having an additional account unattached to the reputation accrued by the individual's other posts or comments on Reddit is common (Leavitt, 2015; Massanari, 2015). These may be temporary "throwaway" accounts or permanent alternate accounts. The practice of having multiple accounts could be seen as an adaptation to Reddit's enforced publicness (there is no private posting setting for Reddit accounts as there is on Facebook) and its default permanence (Costa, 2018; Duffy & Chan, 2019), or as a way to keep context-specific identities discrete when Reddit, like other social media platforms, tends to collapse contexts (Marwick & boyd, 2010; Vitak, 2012). There is no limit to the number of accounts one may have on Reddit, though there is a cost in time and effort associated with establishing and managing multiple accounts.

Posts and comments from some Reddit accounts are generated by automated programs or "bots." The creation and implementation of bot accounts on Reddit is highly context-dependent: most bots are created to execute specific tasks in specific subreddits, such as welcoming new subscribers to the subreddit or reminding potential contributors of the rules of the subreddit (Jhaver et al., 2019; Long et al., 2017). In some cases, these accounts are identified as "bots" either within their usernames (e.g., *u/dataisbeautiful-bot*) or with flair that designates them as a bot. In other cases, they are not identified as such. Bots that fail to identify themselves are often perceived as having violated a norm – discourse on most subreddits is assumed to be the result of spontaneous human interaction.

Identity minimalism

Researchers studying social presence in computer-mediated contexts make distinctions among those contexts based on the presence or absence of social cues such as facial expressions, tone of voice, body language, or attire (Daft & Lengel, 1986; Gunawardena, 1995; Short, Williams, & Christie, 1976; Walther, 1994). A website, application, or platform can offer users any number of cues that provide interlocutors with information as to who people are or how online speech or behavior should be construed. In these frameworks, media or platforms are described as "cue-rich" or "cue-poor" based on both the quality and the quantity of information they provide.

Relative to other popular online social media platforms such as Facebook and YouTube, Reddit is cue-poor, not only in terms of the number of social cues but also in terms of their prominence. Recognizable attributes of a user's identity, such as the username and their karma score, are present but not easy for other users to see while browsing comments and posts. The added time and effort needed to access and process additional identifying information on profile pages distinguishes it from cue-rich platforms in which visual identifying information (e.g., images and videos of the user) makes for rapid and intuitive judgments (Walther, 1994, 2008).

Posting identifiable photos or videos of one's self is not a common practice across all of Reddit, though within certain subreddits (e.g., r/happy), it can be. Doing so attaches the username and the words they write to a body and a face, which often introduces new dimensions to interactions and power dynamics in computer-mediated communication (Walther, Slovacek, & Tidwell, 2001). If the photo or video reveals someone to be attractive or worthy of sympathy, it can have a positive "halo effect" in the form of more upvotes or positive comments. If it is judged to be unattractive or unsympathetic in some way, it can have a corresponding negative effect. Even an image that is judged positively can result in a negative outcome for the user in the form of unwanted romantic or sexual attention.

For most Reddit contributors, identities are conveyed through words, with all other traces of identity – facial expressions, tone of voice, skin tone – stripped away. Much like users of message boards and chat rooms of the 1990s (O'Brien, 1999; Turkle, 1995), contributors generate recognizable identities through gradual accretions of utterances. Discourse analysis – a methodological and theoretical lens through which online commentary is often examined – holds that individuals' true identities are revealed through interactions with others (Gee, 2004). To understand who we are, we must examine what we say to one another.

There are three means by which posts or comments can convey aspects of identity: overt disclosures (e.g., stating that one identifies as a woman), expressions of opinions or experiences (corresponding to Erving Goffman's "impression given"; 1959), and unintended impressions revealed by one's use of language (corresponding to Goffman's "impression given off"). The extent to which identity is expressed in a given post or comment depends on the type of post or comment. Self-posts are most apt to overtly convey aspects of identity. A self-post that tells a story about one's life may disclose a detail about the contributor's identity in order to provide detail or context. When overt disclosures are absent, stories may still give users some sense of who the contributor is, what kind of life they lead, or how they react to different situations. Posts featuring "original content" (OC) – be it a photo, a drawing, or a song created by the contributor – convey something of the contributor's identity, though not as transparently as is the case with self-posts.

Humorous image macros – words superimposed on images, referred to colloquially within Reddit as "memes[3]" – are among the most popular original content posts. Memes involve a process of reappropriating content from one context, modifying or adding to it, and deploying it in another context (Jenkins, Ford, & Green, 2013; Leppänen et al., 2014; Milner, 2016). The juxtaposition of the image's original context with its new context is often part of the humor. Particular image templates are often popular for a limited time, passing through predictable cycles of variations before being superseded by new popular templates (Milner, 2016).

Whether memes are equivalent to utterances in terms of what they convey about the "speaker" isn't obvious. On the one hand, memes are typically presented in posts as content in the same way that a cartoon intended to amuse others or express a political opinion is a piece of content. This positions memes as something to be *talked about* rather than as a part of an ongoing conversation, similar to the way that Twitter positions tweets as outward-facing statements or questions to be discussed in replies which are positioned below the tweets.

On the other hand, memes often convey meaning in a more informal manner than other forms of content. Jean Burgess's concept of "vernacular creativity" is relevant here, as a way of understanding memes' role in Reddit's discourse and culture (2006). Whether we treat memes as texts or discourse, their use of texts depicting *and created by* other people effaces authorship in a way that neither institutional creativity nor everyday conversation does. Despite this effacement, memes reflect the particular sensibilities and values of their creators. In the absence of visual markers of identity and offline reputations, one's tastes and modes of self-expression fill the vacuum to create a social self (Baym, 2015).

Even in the case of self-posts that make overt identity disclosures, other users may not be able to recall the contributor's username after having read the post. This is likely the product of a lack of identity cue prominence as well as how infrequently a single user dominates self-post popularity in larger subreddits. Unlike the practice of linking to others' content, a practice that tends to be dominated by a handful of karma-rich power users within a given subreddit, self-posts tend to originate from many users with very little karma. This suggests that Reddit users do not value diversity of perspectives and taste when it comes to content foraging, but do value it when it comes to reading about others' life experiences. As a result of low identity cue prominence and the large number of contributors posting self-posts (too many to hold in one's mind as discrete people), self-posts are likely to blend together in the minds and memories of their readers, seen not as the product of particular individuals but rather as a disembodied collective voice.

The primacy of text

With its emphasis on text, Reddit resembles another popular social media platform: Twitter. Both platforms started as text-only, later allowing users to post images and video. Even when they were given the abilities to post images and video, contributors to both platforms tended to post pictures and videos in which other people were the subjects, forgoing the opportunity to reveal their own identities in the way that many contributors to YouTube, Instagram, and other image-first platforms commonly do. Contributors to both platforms were still expected to use text to provide some context or commentary on the image or video; on Reddit, this takes the form of a post's title.

Reddit's voting mechanism exerts a subtler influence on the relationship between identity and text. Because Reddit sorts every utterance based on vote score, which in turn affects the visibility of those utterances, it is hard for contributors to escape entirely from the desire not just to convey meaning – what one truly means to say – but to also attempt to garner positive attention from others. Like most social media platforms that tie visibility to popularity, Reddit can train users to express opinions and experiences that appeal to others. But here, it is important to remember Reddit's modularity. While contributors to other platforms compete for the votes of a single, amorphous constituency, contributors to Reddit post to particular subreddits, each with its own constituency. Garnering upvotes and the increased visibility they bring about is a matter of appealing to the sensibilities of particular groups which vary greatly in terms of ideologies and tastes, not unlike the way people "play to the room" in other social contexts (Goffman, 1959; Marwick & boyd, 2011; Turkle, 1995).

Beyond the content of what is said or posted, use of language and grammar can convey something about one's identity, such as age, education level, or nationality of the user. Reddit is primarily in English. Subreddits in other languages date back to the first subreddits, but only one (r/de, written primarily in German) really took root and developed into a popular, sustained community. As elsewhere on the internet, non-native English speaking Redditors are often required to adapt in order to reach a global audience (Barton & Lee, 2012; Seargeant & Tagg, 2014).

Researchers have found that Reddit contributors' uses of certain words correlate with demographic characteristics such as age (Chew et al., 2021), race (Flesch, 2018), and gender (Thelwall & Stuart, 2019), findings that are consistent with research establishing relationships between demographic characteristics and language use in other online contexts (Herring, 2003; Wolf, 2000). Even offline, different groups of people use language in ways that are particular to those groups (Romaine, 2003) though online contexts influence this dynamic in unique ways (Turkle, 1995). Susan Herring's extensive research on emotion, gender, and computer-mediated communication provides useful historical context. As early online social spaces came to be dominated by men, online rhetoric often possessed an adversarial, exclusionary tone for which male contributors were largely responsible (Herring, 1993, 1994, 2003). Despite the subsequent increased adoption of social media by girls and women, language gender dynamics such as those described by Herring persist (Vickery & Everbach, 2018).

While the way we use words corresponds to aspects of our identities, they are not perfectly correlated with them. Definitions of the aforementioned demographic categories, and the observable traits to which they correspond, are fluid, changing across time and across cultures and subcultures. Most social contexts provide a number of observable traits that inform our perceptions of one another's categorical identities, for better or worse. The absence of nearly all of those traits from Reddit's discourse does not render categories of offline identity irrelevant or obsolete. In the text-rich, cue-poor social context of Reddit, a contributor's use of language takes on an outsized importance for other users who, for a variety of reasons, are intent on establishing whether or not the contributor belongs to a particular offline identity category.

A desire for authenticity

On April 1, 2019, moderators of r/BlackPeopleTwitter implemented a new policy. To post a comment or post in the subreddit, contributors had to submit evidence to the moderators that they were, indeed, Black. Thousands of potential contributors sent photos of their forearms to the moderators.

The policy change started as an experiment (Harmon, 2019). Over the years, April 1 – April Fool's Day – has become a day for playful temporary experimentation with Reddit's design and functionality, at first by the administrators and then by moderators of specific subreddits. While r/BlackPeopleTwitter's new policy was initially interpreted as part of this tradition, the moderators' explanation for its adoption made clear that it was meant to serve a more serious purpose.[4] It's implementation, which was continued in a modified form after April Fool's Day ended, was intended to address a problematic dynamic that is not unique to Reddit.

For much of American history, economies of popular culture have exhibited a persistent dynamic of cultural appropriation in which White audiences adopt the vernacular of Black performers and, in doing so, exploit Black culture for gains in cultural and economic capital. Many online spaces which initially held the promise of becoming places where people of different races and ethnicities could form new kinds of communities instead replicated the old dynamic between privileged and marginalized cultures on a global scale (Nakamura, 2013; Song, 2009). Under the protective cover of anonymity, White audiences continued to consume Non-white cultures, this time on platforms with economic models that often failed to compensate content producers in any way (hooks, 1992).

In online social spaces, the dynamic extends from the consumption of culture to the performance and embodiment of it. Lisa Nakamura's concept of "identity tourism" is a valuable lens through which to examine this dynamic as it plays out on Reddit. The term refers to the adoption of another identity online for purposes of exploration and amusement (Nakamura, 2013). When embodying this adopted identity threatens to have negative consequences, "tourists" are free to walk away from it in a way that those born with such identities are not. Being able to convincingly adopt another identity requires certain levels of cultural knowledge, access to cultural goods, and leisure time, making it easier for some users to "pass" as other identities online than it is for others. Even when members of historically marginalized groups have access to those resources and are thus able to convincingly exchange their identities for ones that are perceived in a more positive light, the act can have negative social and political implications for that group. To pass as another type is to efface one's own cultural history, thereby reinforcing social hierarchies and tacitly acknowledging that one identity is more desirable than another (Nakamura, 2013).

Online identity verification policies such as the one implemented by the moderators of r/BlackPeopleTwitter have roots in a long history of authorities using the physical body to authenticate identity (Foucault, 1977). But in this iteration, there is a new twist. The authorities enacting verification practices and exerting power over discourse are members of a historically marginalized group seeking to carve out a space that is free of the kinds of hostility, bigotry, and co-optation of culture that have plagued open online forums since the dawn of the internet (Keum & Miller, 2018).

Authorities' repeated attempts to verify identity and use this information to control discourse, offline and online, are a testament to the importance of identities in public discourse. Despite the absence of bodies, identities relating to bodies have a way of re-asserting themselves in the language used by Reddit contributors (Nakamura, 2013, p. 31). Culture is still represented in the preferences, expressions, and experiences of Reddit's users, though there is more fluidity to identity categories, and expectations of other users are undeniably altered by the absence of social cues. The ability of different groups, including members of historically marginalized groups, to hold positions of authority is a function of Reddit's modularity. In its trajectory, the story of r/BlackPeopleTwitter is common among popular subreddits: there is a crisis (often precipitated in some way by the affordance of anonymity and by growth) and, through moderators' enacting of restrictions, the community adapts.

Notes

1 In 2020, small images or "avatars" began being displayed above user's comments. Users could upload images or select from a range of customizable cartoon avatars modeled after Reddit's alien mascot, Snoo.
2 Often, this is done by celebrities or public figures who use Reddit.
3 The term "meme" was originally intended to refer to an idea that propagated through populations in a way that was analogous to gene propagation (Dawkins, 1976). It then came to refer to short linguistic, image, audio, or video texts that are transformed and shared online (Milner, 2016). Image macros are, strictly speaking, a sub-genre of this broader category, though within Reddit, "memes" is often used in reference to image macros.
4 https://www.reddit.com/r/BlackPeopleTwitter/comments/b82bq9/announcement_blackpeopletwitter_is_now_for_black/

References

Barton, D., & Lee, C. K. (2012). Redefining vernacular literacies in the age of Web 2.0. *Applied Linguistics, 33*(3), 282–298.
Baym, N. K. (2015). *Personal connections in the digital age*. Cambridge, MA: Polity Press.
Brock, A. (2012). From the blackhand side: Twitter as a cultural conversation. *Journal of Broadcasting & Electronic Media, 56*(4), 529–549.
Burgess, J. (2006). Hearing ordinary voices: Cultural studies, vernacular creativity and digital storytelling. *Continuum, 20*(2), 201–214.
Butler, J. (1988). Performative acts and gender constitution: An essay in phenomenology and feminist theory. *Theatre Journal, 40*(4), 519–531.
Chew, R., Kery, C., Baum, L., Bukowski, T., Kim, A., & Navarro, M. (2021). Predicting age groups of Reddit users based on posting behavior and metadata: Classification model development and validation. *JMIR Public Health and Surveillance, 7*(3), 14–40.
Costa, E. (2018). Affordances-in-practice: An ethnographic critique of social media logic and context collapse. *New Media & Society, 20*(10), 3641–3656.
Daft, R. L., & Lengel, R. H. (1986). Organizational information requirements, media richness and structural design. *Management Science, 32*(5), 554–571.
Dawkins, R. (1976). *The selfish gene*. Oxford: Oxford University Press.

Duffy, B. E., & Chan, N. K. (2019). "You never really know who's looking": Imagined surveillance across social media platforms. *New Media & Society, 21*(1), 119–138.
Flesch, M. (2019). "That spelling tho": A sociolinguistic study of the nonstandard form of though in a corpus of Reddit comments. *European Journal of Applied Linguistics, 7*(2), 163–188.
Foucault, M. (1977). *Discipline and punish: The birth of the prison.* New York City: Pantheon.
Gee, J. P. (2004). *An introduction to discourse analysis: Theory and method.* New York: Routledge.
Goffman, E. (1959). *The presentation of self in everyday life.* New York City: Doubleday.
Gunawardena, C. N. (1995). Social presence theory and implications for interaction and collaborative learning in computer conferences. *International Journal of Educational Telecommunications, 1*(2), 147–166.
Haraway, D. (1991). *Simians, cyborgs and women: The reinvention of nature.* London: Free Association.
Harmon, A. (2019, October 8). Discussing blackness on Reddit? Photograph your forearm first. *The New York Times.* https://www.nytimes.com/2019/10/08/us/reddit-race-black-people-twitter.html
Herring, S. C. (1993). Gender and democracy in computer-mediated communication. *Electronic Journal of Communication, 3*(2). http://www.cios.org/EJCPUBLIC/003/2/00328.HTML
Herring, S. C. (1994). Politeness in computer culture: Why women thank and men flame. In M. Bucholtz, A. Liang & L. Sutton (Eds.) *Cultural performances: Proceedings of the third berkeley women and language conference* (pp. 278–294). Berkeley, CA: Berkeley Women and Language Group.
Herring, S. C. (2003). Gender and power in on-line communication. In J. Holmes & M. Meyerhoff (Eds.) *The handbook of language and gender* (pp. 202–228). Malden, MA: Blackwell Publishing.
hooks, b. (1992). *Black looks: Race and representation.* London: Turnaround.
Jenkins, H., Ford, S., & Green, J. (2013). *Spreadable media.* New York: New York University Press.
Jhaver, S., Birman, I., Gilbert, E., & Bruckman, A. (2019). Human-machine collaboration for content regulation: The case of Reddit Automoderator. *ACM Transactions on Computer-Human Interaction (TOCHI), 26*(5), 1–35.
Keum, B. T., & Miller, M. J. (2018). Racism on the internet: Conceptualization and recommendations for research. *Psychology of Violence, 8*(6), 782.
Leavitt, A. (2015, February). "This is a throwaway account": Temporary technical identities and perceptions of anonymity in a massive online community. In *Proceedings of the 18th ACM conference on computer supported cooperative work & social computing* (pp. 317–327). Vancouver, BC: Association for Computing Machinery.
Leppänen, S., Kytölä, S., Jousmäki, H., Peuronen, S., & Westinen, E. (2014). Entextualization and resemiotization as resources for identification in

social media. In P. Seargeant & C. Tagg (Eds.) *The language of social media: Identity and community on the internet* (pp. 112–136). New York: Palgrave Macmillan.

Long, K., Vines, J., Sutton, S., Brooker, P., Feltwell, T., Kirman, B., Barnett, J., & Lawson, S. (2017, May). "Could You Define That in Bot Terms"? Requesting, creating and using bots on Reddit. In *Proceedings of the 2017 CHI conference on human factors in computing systems* (pp. 3488–3500). Denver, CO: Association for Computing Machinery.

Marwick, A. E., & boyd, D. (2011). I tweet honestly, I tweet passionately: Twitter users, context collapse, and the imagined audience. *New Media & Society, 13*(1), 114–133.

Massanari, A. (2015). *Participatory culture, community, and play: Learning from Reddit*. New York: Peter Lang.

Milner, R. M. (2016). *The world made meme: Public conversations and participatory media*. Information Society Series. Cambridge, MA: MIT Press.

Nakamura, L. (2013). *Cybertypes: Race, ethnicity, and identity on the Internet*. New York: Routledge.

O'Brien, J. (1999). Writing in the body: Gender (re)production in online interaction. In P. Kollock & M. Smith (Eds.) *Communities in cyberspace* (pp. 76–106). London: Routledge.

Romaine, S. (2003). Variation in language and gender. In J. Holmes & M. Meyerhoff (Eds.) *The handbook of language and gender* (pp. 98–118). Malden, MA: Blackwell Publishing.

Ryan, R. M., & Deci, E. L. (2012). Multiple identities within a single self. In M. R. Leary & J. P. Tangney (Eds.) *Handbook of self and identity* (pp. 225–246). New York: The Guilford Press.

Seargeant, P., & Tagg, C. (Eds.). (2014). *The language of social media: Identity and community on the internet*. New York: Palgrave Macmillan.

Short, J., Williams, E., & Christie, B. (1976). *The social psychology of telecommunications*. New York: Wiley.

Song, F. W. (2009). *Virtual communities: Bowling alone, online together*. New York: Peter Lang.

Thelwall, M., & Stuart, E. (2019). She's Reddit: A source of statistically significant gendered interest information?. *Information Processing & Management, 56*(4), 1543–1558.

Turkle, S. (1995). *Life on the screen: Identity in the age of the internet*. New York: Simon & Schuster.

Vickery, J. R., & Everbach, T. (Eds.) (2018). *Mediating misogyny*. New York: Palgrave Macmillan.

Vitak, J. (2012). The impact of context collapse and privacy on social network site disclosures. *Journal of Broadcasting & Electronic Media, 56*(4), 451–470.

Walther, J. B. (1994). Anticipated ongoing interaction versus channel effects on relational communication in computer-mediated interaction. *Human Communication Research, 20*(4), 473–501.

Walther, J. B. (2008). Social information processing theory. In D. O. Braithwaite & P. Schrodt (Eds.) *Engaging theories in interpersonal communication: Multiple perspectives* (pp. 417–428).

Walther, J. B., Slovacek, C. L., & Tidwell, L. C. (2001). Is a picture worth a thousand words? Photographic images in long-term and short-term computer-mediated communication. *Communication Research*, *28*(1), 105–134.

Wolf, A. (2000). Emotional expression online: Gender differences in emoticon use. *Cyberpsychology & Behavior*, *3*(5), 827–833.

5 Reddit and democracy

If you gave a few hundred million people the ability to create online communities from scratch, what kinds of communities would they create? The common topics and uses of the millions of communities on Reddit are reviewed in Chapter 2, but this leaves unanswered the question of how subreddits are governed. There is a long-standing bias against bureaucratic, interventionist leadership on the internet, both because it violates core values of early internet adopters and because, at least prior to the development of increasingly advanced moderation bots in the late 2010s, such leadership was difficult to scale up. This meant that most subreddit moderators took a laissez-faire approach to the tasks of leadership, letting constituents determine the worth of a post or comment by using the upvote and downvote buttons. And if the purpose or character of the subreddit gradually drifted or suddenly diverged from its original purpose or character, so be it; it was the will of the people.

As Reddit grew, the shortcomings of this approach became more evident. Content posted to many subreddits quickly became repetitive. In many mid-size subreddits, a handful of contributors became highly attuned to what constituents upvoted and cranked out post after post conforming to those narrow desires, sapping the subreddit of any originality. Constituents' self-policing of spam, off-topic rants, and hostile comments via voting didn't work as well when subreddits were new and small. There were too few constituents to bury such posts and comments in downvotes, and so these contributions clogged up content feeds and discourse, yielding an unwelcoming, unappealing destination for curious explorers, preventing the subreddit from growing.

Giving moderators the ability to address these shortcomings through intervention raises questions: Who grants them this power? Are there any limits to it? What recourse do users have if a moderator abuses it? Most subreddits are run as "benign oligarchies" by several

DOI: 10.4324/9781003150800-5

moderators who are not elected but rather appointed by existing moderators (creators of subreddits are their original moderators by default). Moderators know that if they run afoul of their constituents and contributors, splinter subreddits will arise and users will leave. Coups – in which one or several new moderators seize power, expelling old moderators and changing the character of the subreddit – are not unheard of, but most subreddits manage to exist peacefully, tolerating laissez-faire leadership and its aforementioned shortcomings.

This is not the case on r/IndiaSpeaks. This relatively small subreddit dedicated to anything relating to the country of India has several mechanisms for generating original, insightful commentary, including a regularly scheduled debate of timely topics, "cultural exchanges" with subreddits dedicated to other countries, and an India-specific "Ask Me Anything" series in which prominent Indians are interviewed by r/IndiaSpeaks contributors. These events are organized by the r/IndiaSpeaks council, a "middle-level group (Between the community and the Mod team) of 10 users which helps promote activity, resolve serious conflicts, organize events and other roles."[1] The council is composed of a balance of moderator-appointed users and members elected by a two-thirds majority vote in quarterly subreddit-wide elections.

Both the common laissez-faire approach to leadership and r/IndiaSpeaks' uncommon power-sharing structure could be considered "democracies." They serve as a reminder of how broadly we often define the term "democracy" as well as how flexible subreddits are in terms of their social and power structure. Reddit is a kind of laboratory for democracy in which various structures of power can be tested. This chapter considers what these experiments in democracy have yielded. The chapter is also about political communication more broadly: how individuals and groups with various ideologies support, debate, and compete with one another online.

Definitions of democracy

Democracy is a form of government in which the people determine the laws that govern society, either directly – by proposing and/or voting on laws – or indirectly – by electing officials who then propose and vote on laws on the people's behalf. Democracy is also a process, one that typically includes deliberation (i.e., thinking and discussion) relating to public issues. In certain societies, democracy has also become a kind of abstract, inherently positive value – like freedom or fairness. This view of democracy selectively emphasizes parts of the democratic process while de-emphasizing others. Voting is synonymous with the idealized democracy while deliberation is often ignored, perhaps because the former is easier to define and measure. Indirect democracy necessitates the existence of politicians, a group toward which many democracy enthusiasts remain distinctly unenthused. Reddit arose from a culture that is not only democratic in governance, but also holds this view of democracy as a value.

Political philosophers have long wrestled with questions about the roles of deliberation and representation in democracies. Plato's critiques of "mob rule" articulated an early skepticism toward direct democracy. Crowds, according to Plato, are subject to impulses, are not prone to arriving at decisions favoring the common good, and are apt to mistake anarchy for freedom (Jowett, 1888). Montesquieu and Rousseau worried about popular elections of representatives, rather than favoring the smartest or the most capable of leading, might instead favor privileged aristocrats and those with strong personalities. James Madison, writing in the Federalist Papers, draws from these critiques in making a case against direct democracy.

The popularization of mass media – newsprint, radio, and television – inspired a new wave of writing on democracy (e.g., Dewey, 1927; Lippmann, 1922). By that point, democracy had been implemented in much of the Western World, and most of the writing tended to focus less on democracy's complexities and drawbacks and more on threats to democracy. Rapid urbanization and industrialization brought people into close proximity with one another, but rather than discuss experiences and perspectives with their neighbors and co-workers, citizens of modern societies tended to passively consume news and opinions on public matters published and broadcast via mass media. The effect was a public opinion bereft of deliberation, subject to manipulation by the small group of powerful people who controlled mass media production.

Meanwhile, a wide variety of democracies with varying degrees of directness and deliberation have flourished. Small towns in New England continue to hold open town meetings – a form of direct democracy – well into the 21st century. U.S. presidential primary caucuses in the state of Iowa typically include intense public deliberation immediately prior to the voting process. Nearly 2 billion individuals live in countries with some form of parliamentary democracy, in which large popularly elected legislative bodies hold ultimate power. Democracy is as popular a form of government as it has ever been (DeSilver, 2019), but few if any of these governments live up to the idealized vision of democracy. Lobbying, conflict, and partisanship are as synonymous with democracy as voting and deliberation, and participation rates in all parts of the democratic process in many Western democracies remain far from ideal. For example, 48% of the United States population voted in the 2020 presidential election (cfr.org, 2020).

All of this serves as a reminder that democracy has always been, for lack of a better term, "messy," both in theory and in practice. Democracy's messiness – its complexity, diversity, and weaknesses – tends to be least evident when democracies are being compared favorably to alternative forms of rule (e.g., dictatorship) or when they are (or are perceived to be) under assault.

Democracy online

Democracy, as it is depicted in early utopian accounts of virtual communities, is an ideal arrangement in which power is evenly distributed and everyone has equal voice. Whereas mass media had been cast as an impediment to realizing this ideal, the internet had the potential to correct the acknowledged shortcomings of democracies in the offline world (Rheingold, 1993). Online anonymity would sever the connection between one's station in life and the deference paid to them in discussions of public affairs, preventing the wealthy and powerful from dominating discourse and wielding undue influence. Voices of individuals living far from cultural, governmental, and financial centers would be weighted equally to those emanating from elite institutions. Participation in discussions on public affairs would no longer be the sole domain of professional pundits. A new era of widespread civic engagement would dawn. Provided internet access could be widely and evenly distributed, more people would have more power.

Beyond that, details about the relationship between online discussions of public affairs and the distribution of power offline were scarce. Song (2009) and Hindman (2009) note that while there is a lot of talk about the democratizing potential of online communities, there is little clarity about what "democratic" means in this context. The early message boards from which scholars extrapolated exhibited many of the longed-for attributes of democracy: flattened hierarchies, spirited debate, power sharing. But at the time scholars began writing about the democratizing potential of the internet, internet users were, despite some geographic diversity, a largely homogenous group: well educated and well off. Text-only discussion forums lacked the sensory-saturated feel that defined television and would return in subsequent iterations of the online public sphere.

Zizi Papacharissi's concept of "affective publics" is a useful framework for understanding how democracy and power operate in the era of mass internet adoption (2015). Affective publics manifest themselves within "third spaces" that are not explicitly designated as entirely public or private, commercial or personal, work or leisure, but are instead hybrid spaces (p. 25). They are "affective" in the sense that they encourage expressions of emotion and feeling, deviating from the dispassionate rationality to which many legacy news organizations and governments aspired. By acknowledging the role that affect plays in debates of public affairs, we can start to make sense of discussions in which the introduction of new information does little to change people's minds, basic facts are highly contested, and online arguments boil over into the offline world.

Any consideration of democracy online must also include an account of how citizens are informed about public affairs. The shift from top-down models of news distribution – in which editors, producers, and television network executives determine which ideas were circulated – to bottom-up viral or "spreadable" media distribution (Jenkins, Green, & Ford, 2013) – in which individual users' actions (e.g., emailing, "liking," sharing) determine content's visibility – changed the economics of journalism (detailed in Chapter 7) and altered the landscape of reporting on public affairs. Taking part[2] of the editorial process out of the hands of "the elite" and putting it in the hands of "the people" could easily be characterized as "democratizing" (Wihbey, 2014), but it is also a process of "affectizing": increasing the incentive to appeal to users' emotions. News articles with headlines evoking strong emotions were more likely to be shared by users because they spoke to deep-seated urges: to identify, avoid, or mitigate threats to one's affinity group; to avoid social isolation (Brewer, 2007; Cacioppo et al., 2011).

In a news environment increasingly constructed by users' immediate impulses, deliberative democracy gave way to *impulsive democracy*. Deliberative democracy comes not just with debate among people who are not like-minded, but also with *time*. The process of deliberation involves mulling over ideas, not just debating them. In a deliberative democracy, voting takes place *after* lengthy discussion, debate, and – at least ideally – consideration. In the large-scale, impulsive online democracies that reconfigured discussions of public affairs, of which Reddit was among the first, judgment is rendered instantly, without thought, on impulse.

Such an account gives us some idea of how a technology that solicits active participation from billions of users has failed to live up to high-minded ideals that the word "democracy" inspires, but it risks effacing individual differences among platforms, websites, or, in Reddit's case, subreddits. To understand how Reddit operates as a collection of democracies, we must take a closer look at its design and communities.

Democracies within Reddit

Several attributes common to democracies have corresponding analogs on Reddit. Most obviously, there is voting on posts and comments. As noted in the introductory chapter, the main purpose of voting is to increase (with an upvote) or decrease (with a downvote) the visibility of a post or comment. As subreddits eclipsed the general-purpose reddit.com homepage (see Chapter 2 for a timeline), initial voting constituencies for a post or comment were likely to be those who subscribed to the subreddit to which the post or comment was contributed.

If a post or comment achieves enough upvotes in a short enough span of time, it will rise to the top of a "hot" list within the subreddit and/or be featured on r/all or r/popular which are visible to a greater number of users, many of whom do not subscribe to the subreddit to which the post was contributed. The precise number of votes required to reach these lists is not known to users. Additionally, the actual vote scores displayed next to posts do not precisely reflect the number of upvotes minus the number of downvotes as one would expect, but are rather an approximation of it. This "vote fuzzing" is intended to frustrate those seeking to manipulate vote scores via automated bots by withholding feedback as to whether the manipulation attempt is achieving its goal.

This lack of transparency in voting would likely not be tolerated in an offline democracy, nor would the practice of unelected moderators removing posts or comments they deem to be in violation of the subreddit's rules without the knowledge of most users. Why are these apparently "undemocratic" practices tolerated on Reddit? Many users are likely unaware of vote fuzzing and of the number of posts and comments removed by moderators, many of which are irrelevant spam. Moreover, whether or not a particular post is featured on r/all or r/popular is of little consequence to a casual user who merely seeks effective diversions, or to an experienced user who likely eschews these public-facing aggregated pages for the curated list of links comprised of the subreddits to which they subscribe. What might be regarded as an unacceptable lack of transparency in another context is an implicit acknowledgement of the imperfections of democracy online, particularly the persistent presence of "bad actors" seeking to manipulate the voting process.

Discussions of public affairs on Reddit roughly resemble the discourse on message boards of the 20th-century internet with one key difference: voting on comments. The same mechanism that weeds out most irrelevant comments and increases the visibility of appealing comments is thought to create "echo chambers" of public opinion. According to this view, constituents upvote comments expressing opinions with which they agree and downvote ones with which they don't, regardless of the merit or quality of the comments. This makes opinions diverging from the majority less apt to be seen. Contributors seeking positive attention may, consciously or not, "play to the crowd" while users posting minority opinions are apt to become frustrated and to stop contributing to the subreddit, leading to a "spiral of silence" in which minority voices become fewer and fewer (Noelle-Neumann, 1993). Even without the voting mechanism, modular platforms like Reddit that create discrete spaces for specific topics and sub-topics have a tendency to attract those who share a perspective on public matters, unlike the sprawling, undifferentiated public spheres of Facebook, YouTube, and Twitter (McEwan, Carpenter, & Hopke, 2018; Weeks, Ksiazek, & Holbert, 2016). The ability to vote on comments likely exacerbates this tendency.

To lessen these effects, many subreddits temporarily hide vote scores. The first few votes on a post or comment tend to be predictive of its eventual score – a "rich-get-richer" effect that is likely more pronounced in larger subreddits, where low-scoring posts or comments are quickly buried under new contributions. Vote scores are "social information": easy-to-process indicators of what others approve of, something humans are prone to pay attention to (Cialdini, 1984; Cooley, 1909). Hiding vote scores reduces this information but does not eliminate it; posts and comments are still ranked by votes, so hiding vote scores merely eliminates information about the vote discrepancy between ranked posts.

A few subreddits have created alternative ways of ranking posts. In r/changemyview, users can award comments that make substantive, convincing arguments with a "Delta" vote. The substantiveness and convincingness of arguments are verified by other users and moderators.[3] By default, comments in the subreddit are sorted in such a way that comments with the most deltas are most visible. This alternative allocation of visibility privileges substantive arguments over confirmatory snark, and typically yields an optimal discourse on controversial topics: civil, well-reasoned, and supported by evidence. r/bestof allows users to submit self-posts or comments that they find to be worthy of enshrinement in the subreddit's archive, and though the subreddit's rules do not stipulate that submissions must relate to arguments about public affairs, they often do. In effect, the subreddit is a way of bookmarking particularly substantive, persuasive arguments (e.g., a contributor's critique of the phrase "All Lives Matter," which was cited by news websites [Boingboing.net, 2015; Vox.com, 2016] as an example of a convincing argument in defense of the *Black Lives Matter* movement).

The successes of r/changemyview and r/bestof in generating and cataloging high-quality deliberation prompt the questions: why are these moderately popular subreddits not more popular, and why are their techniques for generating high-quality discourse not more widely adopted across the site? Though a lack of awareness of these subreddits may be part of the cause, there may also be a dearth of demand. Here, we must acknowledge the gulf between the democratic possibilities of widespread internet adoption and its realities. The vast majority of Reddit users do not contribute to subreddits relating to public affairs, the discourse of which tends to be dominated by relatively few contributors. For example, during the month of April 2015, roughly 1.3% of r/Politics's 3.1 million subscribers contributed a comment on the subreddit. Of those commenters, 10% accounted for 82% of the total vote scores for comments in that subreddit during that month. Similarly, roughly 1.8% of r/news's 5.3 million subscribers commented that month, 10% of whom accounted for 85% of the total vote score.

This low participation rate is not unique to Reddit (Hughes & Asheer, 2019). Despite the ease with which users may participate in public affairs discussions online, relatively few do. To understand the motivations of those who participate in Reddit's discourse on public affairs and the lack of demand for subreddit functions that cultivate robust debate, we must avoid considering it in a vacuum and turn our attention to the ways in which behavior on Reddit intersects with broader economic and cultural realities (Bail, 2021). In particular, we must consider the ways in which highly motivated political activists use Reddit and other platforms to affect change.

Political movements on Reddit

The actions of most political movements online are not "democratic" in the sense of giving equal weight to every voice within the movement. Rather, they create alternative public spheres intended to compensate for what their participants see as an unfair lack of representation of their perspectives in mainstream public discourse. Their expressions often take the form of strategic communication: attempts to use media technologies to reach broader audiences and persuade others (often those with influence, like journalists or high-profile bloggers or podcasters) to be more sympathetic toward their cause (Martinez-Torres, 2001; Russell, 2001). Whereas the centralized nature of traditional mass media production and distribution prevented smaller, less mainstream groups from reaching large audiences, the decentralized nature of masspersonal[4] technologies makes it harder for those in power to effectively regulate the speech of these groups, allowing them to reach larger audiences and to call into question the legitimacy of those in power (Karmack & Nye, 2002).

Online movements are large, loose networks that organize quickly (Hindman, 2009). As Papacharissi notes (2015), many of these movements are ideologically shapeless and organizationally fluid: leaders and manifestos are evident, but no single, mutually agreed-upon edicts persist, and no mechanism for decision-making is codified. The web imposes its logic on all movements: lowering the barrier to entry, accelerating all processes. The list of political or quasi-political movements born or nurtured online is, by 2021, quite long: *The Occupy Movement, The Umbrella Movement, The Tea Party, Anonymous, BlackLivesMatter, Brexit, MeToo*, as well as avid supporters of U.S. presidential candidates Howard Dean, Ron Paul, Bernie Sanders, and Donald Trump. The role of Twitter in the Arab Spring uprisings of 2010–2012 is perhaps the most commonly cited example of digital activism likely because the outcome was, to that point, the biggest political shift of the networked era (Howard & Hussain, 2013).

Since then, online political activism has yielded a wide variety of outcomes: giving prominence to a formerly marginalized perspective; making a formerly obscure, reputable movement appear unhinged and violent; solidifying a voting bloc that helps elect a candidate; appearing efficacious at first but having little or no demonstrable long-term impact. This variety of outcomes confirms the limitations of a technologically deterministic view. The use of social media does not guarantee the success of grassroots political movements formed and nurtured online; rather, it is part of a larger collection of forces – political, economic, sociocultural – that, together, determine impact (Papacharissi, 2015).

As the novelty of online activism wore off, scholarly research tended to consider online movements within the contexts of offline life. Much of the second wave of scholarship on the democratic potential of the internet (2000–2010) tended to focus on inequalities of participation in online discourse (e.g., Mossberger, Tolbert, & Stansbury, 2003; Sylvester & McGlynn, 2010). Scholars were quick to note how White men were overrepresented online, fearing that unless access were expanded, existing inequalities in the offline public sphere would be replicated online (Fairlie, 2004; Hargittai, 2003). This account of the "digital divide," while undeniably true, ignores class – not just as an economic category but as a cultural one. Class separates the highly educated White men who dominated early online political discourse from the less well-educated, underemployed White men who would become active online in the 2010s, just as Reddit was growing in popularity (Pew Research Center, 2021).

Felicia Wu Song (2009) notes that early understandings of virtual communities, like those of Howard Rheingold's and other techno-optimists of the 1990s, imagined them to exist in a cultural vacuum, fundamentally apart from face-to-face communities (p. 74). In reality, technology merely "houses" pre-existing social realities. An expanding online public sphere encompassed groups with long-standing grievances rooted in political and economic realities largely absent from both early online political discourse and most discussions of its potential. The decimation of manufacturing and farming industries by globalization, the collapse of communism and the wave of corruption that filled the subsequent power vacuum, and sectarian civil wars are not merely topics of discussion; they are conditions that shape the worldviews of citizens, often in ways that are abhorrent to others. These voices were "repressed" in the sense that they had largely been excluded from mainstream political discourse. Politicians and journalists were happy to talk *about* those living under such conditions and would occasionally talk *to* them. Seldom would they hand over control to them.

As the platform with a reach that went beyond those of other anonymous or pseudonymous platforms and a structure facilitating the formation of highly coordinated groups that persisted over time (unlike Twitter, which tended to link political allies in looser, transient networks), Reddit became the primary venue through which long-harbored grievances were expressed and acted upon. Reddit's modularity served to cultivate aggrieved political and ideological movements, with homogeneous constituencies suppressing dissenting voices by downvoting them, achieving a kind of ideological purity. Members of the community legitimize and encourage one another provided they adhere to an ideological orthodoxy. Less a venue for discussing public affairs, political movement subreddits function more as a tool for inflaming long-standing grievances, often among the underclasses.

The structure of Reddit discourages users from directly interacting with other users holding opposing views, but this doesn't mean that users are not exposed to expressions of those views. The extent to which online communicative acts, including political communication, are *visible* to others sets computer-mediated communication apart from face-to-face or mass communication (Treem, Leonardi, & van den Hooff, 2020). While the actual person – with all their complexities and personal history – remains obscure, the things they say and, in the era of smartphone recordings, the things they *do* become visible to others in unprecedented ways. The ease with which utterances and actions are replicated and spread across platforms as well as the archived-by-default nature of communication on social networks (boyd, 2010; Ellison & Vitak, 2015) all but ensure that they will be taken out of context.

In the political/ideological arena, this is done strategically, to highlight the most egregious and alarming utterances and actions of one's opponents. Blogs with clear ideological positions (e.g., Breitbart.com; *The Huffington Post*) provide convenient collections of such content, to which these subreddits frequently link in posts (Hoffa, 2017). Authors of the blogs and contributors to these subreddits both engage in a kind of politically motivated information foraging: scanning social media and other information archives, cherry-picking content that confirms one's worst suspicions of ideological opponents, stripping it of context, and using it to foment passion. This use of Reddit can arise spontaneously with minimal coordination or it can be highly orchestrated, necessitating the use of off-site tools such as Discord (an instant messaging platform) and shared spreadsheets (Breland, 2020; Lagorio-Chafkin, 2018; Peck, 2020). Whether this is done merely to vent frustration, to seek support and solidarity, or to recruit and motivate like-minded others likely varies from individual to individual, but the end result is the same: a homogeneous lowlight-reel of bad behavior.

While bloggers and journalists provide commentary that serve to frame ideological opponents' behavior as worthy of derision, Reddit commenters provide an additional frame. In cases in which users merely read the post's title and do not read the accompanying article (which are likely common), Reddit comments are the only frame that users encounter. Comments in such communities contain some of the clearest examples of hate speech on Reddit. Distinct from other forms of hostile speech that target individuals, hate speech targets specific groups – justifying discrimination against them, promoting negative stereotypes about them, or advocating for their extermination (Chandrasekharan et al., 2017; Nockleby, 2000). The increasing frequency of such comments on Reddit forced a kind of prolonged reckoning from 2013 to 2020 in which administrators banned numerous subreddits (Hankes, 2015; Peck, 2020).

It is reasonable to suspect that banning users or subreddits who engage in hate speech merely pushes the behavior to other subreddits or onto other platforms. A 2017 study of Reddit activity after the banning of subreddits detected no discernable uptick in hateful speech across Reddit, suggesting that bans do not merely push bad behavior onto other subreddits (Chandrasekharan et al., 2017). And while platforms such as Voat, Parler, and Gab experienced surges in activity following crackdowns on hate speech on Reddit and other popular social platforms, administrators of these alternative platforms found it difficult to sustain them.

Reddit as public spheres

None of this "messiness" would have surprised political philosopher James Mill. Even absent bad actors who seek to manipulate and mislead, the gathering of those with interests and experiences so disparate from one another, Mill surmised, would make deliberation and debate impossible (Mill, 1829). Were large groups of citizens to engage in debate for the purposes of directly determining the laws of the land, the debates would devolve into violent arguments by way of "mutual inflammation" of feelings. The banning of users and subreddits, and other forms of administrator and moderator intervention, strike many as undemocratic. And yet, absent the widespread adoption of the kind of complex power-sharing mechanisms evident in r/IndiaSpeaks (for which there seems to be little demand), they have been the only effective means of managing the worst instincts of the mutually inflamed. Rules regulating voting and deliberation are nothing new; they are features of nearly every democratic system, seemingly inevitable once a group reaches a certain size. But they are anathema to the ideal of "democracy as a value" on which Reddit was built.

In a sense, Reddit contains three "publics," each one nested in another. The outer layer consists of visitors: those who view and listen to content on the site but do not vote, comment, award, or post. This group may or may not be registered users. They have the least amount of effect on Reddit's discourse and content, and yet they represent the majority of Reddit's users. It is in the administrators' interest to keep them coming back, so as to generate revenue from their exposure to ads on the platform. For this reason, administrators might establish or modify content rules, introduce features, or otherwise alter the site to cater to this group, even if doing so upsets a smaller, more active group of Reddit users.

The second public are constituents: registered users who vote on posts or comments. They are also, by necessity, visitors to the site. These users directly influence the future visibility of content on the site. It is important to remember the size of this group. The most popular Reddit post garnered roughly 350,000 upvotes, a number that is smaller than the population of Aurora, Colorado, the 54th most populous city in the United States. Even if we were to add the number of constituents who downvoted this popular post, the resulting number would still be far less than the total number of visitors to the site. Those who vote on Reddit are not "the people," but rather a small, un-representative sample of Reddit's userbase.

The third public is smaller still – composed of Reddit users who contribute content: either comments or posts. Though they are not required to also vote on content in order to contribute, it is likely that they also engage in this lower-effort behavior. Contributors generate the discourse, but are dependent on voters for their expressions to reach an audience. This likely causes them to cater, consciously or unconsciously, to the preferences of voters.

Arguably, the voice of this third public is just as un-representative of the general public as the individuals in charge of the top-down mass media system it displaces, but just in a different way. Rather than favoring views that support the status quo, there is a systematic bias toward disrupting it. Even when hundreds of millions of users are permitted to speak, intermediaries and hierarchies persist. Those with the technical and cultural savvy, the free time to create and distribute viral opinions, and the ability to tolerate the inevitable emotional abuse that comes with expressing one's opinions online have a greater power to shape discussions of public affairs than those who have only some or none of these attributes.

In a way, Reddit and other popular platforms have centralized public discourse, condensing debates taking place in various town meetings, proverbial coffeehouses and pubs, and local contexts into a smaller number of larger online discussions. Thus condensed, these public debates make for an appealing target for manipulation and coercion, a "one-stop-shop" for anyone seeking to co-opt the voice of the people to suit their own ends. If popular public opinion confers legitimacy in a democracy, then control over popular public opinion is the path to power.

Two key features of political discourse on Reddit are the platform's pseudonymity and interlocutors' remoteness from one another. One may insult another person or group without fear of immediate retaliation. On the battlefield of online public opinion, remote pseudonymous communication is a means of waging asymmetric warfare, making it easier to mete out emotional and psychological damage than it is to defend one's self or others. The lack of social cues make it easier to treat others without empathy, to see utterances and actions as an extension of a threatening group that is increasing in power rather than as expressions of other human beings, despite Reddit's admonition to "remember the human."[5] The fact that such an admonition must be made in the first place suggests that something about Reddit, or perhaps online communication more broadly, has caused some users to forget that they are interacting with other humans.

Of course, in some cases, Reddit users are *not* interacting with other humans. u/CoolDownBot is a bot that encourages contributors who use uncivil language to take a break and cool down. This inspired another Reddit user to create u/FuckCoolDownBot2, a "counter-bot" that automatically responds to u/CoolDownBot's comments with an expletive-laden, hostile rebuttal, to which u/CoolDownBot automatically responds, triggering another response from u/FuckCoolDownBot2. Such interactions are a long way from the models of public debate that Plato or James Mill had in mind, but they serve as examples of the remarkable range of discourse on Reddit, human or otherwise.

Notes

1. https://www.reddit.com/r/IndiaSpeaks/wiki/council?v=7aff9518-5a6a-11e9-9ef3-0ea723a3b3d8&f=flair_name%3A%22%23News%22
2. Editors and executives created the menus of options from which news consumers selected, and in doing so, continued to exert power over discourse about public affairs.
3. https://www.reddit.com/r/changemyview/wiki/deltasystem
4. "Masspersonal" technologies like Twitter, YouTube, and Reddit, allow individuals to reach large audiences (O'Sullivan & Carr, 2018). They stand in contrast to mass media, which allows only a small group of producers to reach large audiences, and personal media, which allows individuals to reach other individuals.
5. https://www.reddit.com/r/blog/comments/1ytp7q/remember_the_human/

References

Bail, C. A. (2021). *Breaking the social media prism: How to make our platforms less polarizing.* Princeton, NJ: Princeton University Press.

Boingboing.net. (2015). Why 'All Lives Matter' instead of 'Black Lives Matter' is such a stupid thing to say. BoingBoing. https://boingboing.net/2015/07/21/why-all-lives-matter-inste.html

boyd, D. (2010). Social network sites as networked publics: Affordances, dynamics, and implications. In Z. Papacharissi (Ed.) *A networked self* (pp. 39–58). New York: Routledge.

Breland, A. (2020). How the most toxic, notorious pro-Trump online community tricked Reddit and got back online. *Mother Jones*. https://www.motherjones.com/politics/2020/10/the_donald_reddit_discord/

Brewer, M. B. (2007). The importance of being we: Human nature and intergroup relations. *American Psychologist, 62*(8), 728.

Cacioppo, J. T., Hawkley, L. C., Norman, G. J., & Berntson, G. G. (2011). Social isolation. *Annals of the New York Academy of Sciences, 1231*(1), 17.

Cfr.org. (2020). The 2020 election by the numbers. Cfr.org. https://www.cfr.org/blog/2020-election-numbers

Chandrasekharan, E., Pavalanathan, U., Srinivasan, A., Glynn, A., Eisenstein, J., & Gilbert, E. (2017). You can't stay here: The efficacy of reddit's 2015 ban examined through hate speech. *Proceedings of the ACM on Human-Computer Interaction, 1*(CSCW), 31.

Cialdini, R. B. (1984). *Influence: Science and practice*. Boston, MA: Pearson.

Cooley, C. H. (1909). *Social organization: A study of the larger mind*. New York: Charles Scribner's Sons.

DeSilver, D. (2019). Despite global concerns about democracy, more than half of countries are democratic. Pew Research Center. https://www.pewresearch.org/fact-tank/2019/05/14/more-than-half-of-countries-are-democratic/

Dewey, J. (1927). *The public and its problems*. New York: Holt.

Ellison, N., & Vitak, J. (2015). Social media affordances and their relationship to social capital processes. In S. Sundar (Ed.), *The handbook of psychology of communication technology* (pp. 205–227). Boston, MA: Wiley-Blackwell.

Fairlie, R. W. (2004). Race and the digital divide. *Contributions in Economic Analysis & Policy, 3*(1), 1–38.

Hankes, K. (2015). How Reddit became a worse black hole of violent racism than stormfront. *Gawker*. https://gawker.com/how-reddit-became-a-worse-black-hole-of-violent-racism-1690505395

Hargittai, E. (2003). The digital divide and what to do about it. In D. C. Jones (Ed.) *New economy handbook* (pp. 821–839). San Diego, CA: Academic Press.

Hindman, M. (2009). *The myth of digital democracy*. Princeton, NJ: Princeton University Press.

Hoffman, F. (2017). Reddit top domains: The news sources that reddit prefers. Medium. https://hoffa.medium.com/reddit-favorite-sources-the-most-linked-sites-expanded-and-interactive-79070d648573

Howard, P. N., & Hussain, M. M. (2013). *Democracy's fourth wave?: Digital media and the Arab Spring*. Oxford: Oxford University Press.

Hughes, A., & Asheer, N. (2019). National politics on Twitter: Small share of US adults produce majority of tweets. Pew Research Center. https://www.pewresearch.org/politics/2019/10/23/national-politics-on-twitter-small-share-of-u-s-adults-produce-majority-of-tweets/

Jenkins, H., Ford, S., & Green, J. (2013). *Spreadable media*. New York: New York University Press.
Jowett, B. (1888). *The Republic of Plato*. Oxford: Clarendon Press.
Karmack, E. C., & Nye, J. S. (2002). *Governance.com: Democracy in the information age*. Spring Hill, NJ: Brookings Institution Press.
Lagorio-Chafkin, C. (2018). *We are the nerds: The birth and tumultuous life of Reddit, the Internet's culture laboratory*. New York: Hachette Books.
Lippmann, W. (1922). *Public opinion*. New York: Harcourt, Brace and Company.
Martinez-Torres, M. E. (2001). Civil society, the Internet, and the Zapatistas. *Peace Review, 13*(3), 347–355.
McEwan, B., Carpenter, C. J., & Hopke, J. E. (2018). Mediated skewed diffusion of issues information: A theory. *Social Media + Society, 4*(3), 2056305118800319.
Mill, J. (1829). *Essays on government, jurisprudence, liberty of the press, and law of nations*. London: J. Innes.
Mossberger, K., Tolbert, C. J., & Stansbury, M. (2003). *Virtual inequality: Beyond the digital divide*. Washington, DC: Georgetown University Press.
Nockleby, J. (2000). Hate speech. In L. Levy and K. Karst (Eds.) *Encyclopedia of the American constitution, Vol. 3, 2nd Edition* (p. 1277). Detroit, MI: Macmillan.
Noelle-Neumann, E. (1993). *The spiral of silence*. Chicago, IL: University of Chicago Press.
O'Sullivan, P. B., & Carr, C. T. (2018). Masspersonal communication: A model bridging the mass-interpersonal divide. *New Media & Society, 20*(3), 1161–1180.
Papacharissi, Z. (2015). *Affective publics: Sentiment, technology, and politics*. Oxford: Oxford University Press.
Peck, R. (2020). The hate-fueled rise of r/The_Donald – and Its Epic Takedown. Wired. https://www.wired.com/story/the-hate-fueled-rise-of-rthe-donald-and-its-epic-takedown/
Pew Research Center. (2021). Internet/Broadband fact sheet. Accessed July 27, 2021, Retrieved from https://www.pewresearch.org/internet/fact-sheet/internet-broadband/?menuItem=d5edf003-5858-4269-89c5-f2889ecf7951
Rheingold, H. (1993). *The virtual community: Homesteading on the electronic frontier*. Reading, MA: Addison-Wesley Publishing.
Russell, A. M. (2001). *Local struggle in a global environment: The Internet and the Zapatista Movement*. Bloomington: Indiana University Press.
Song, F. W. (2009). *Virtual communities: Bowling alone, online together*. New York: Peter Lang.
Sylvester, D. E., & McGlynn, A. J. (2010). The digital divide, political participation, and place. *Social Science Computer Review, 28*(1), 64–74.
Treem, J. W., Leonardi, P. M., & van den Hooff, B. (2020). Computer-mediated communication in the age of communication visibility. *Journal of Computer-Mediated Communication, 25*(1), 44–59.

Vox.com. (2016). Why you should stop saying 'all lives matter,' explained in 9 different ways. Vox.com. https://www.vox.com/2016/7/11/12136140/black-all-lives-matter

Weeks, B. E., Ksiazek, T. B., & Holbert, R. L. (2016). Partisan enclaves or shared media experiences? A network approach to understanding citizens' political news environments. *Journal of Broadcasting & Electronic Media, 60*(2), 248–268.

Wihbey, J. P. (2014, June). The challenges of democratizing news and information: Examining data on social media, viral patterns and digital influence. *Shorenstein Center on Media, Politics and Public Policy Discussion Paper Series, #D-85.*

6 Reddit as community

Throughout the previous chapters of this book, I've used a word – "community" – without properly defining it. I used the word as a kind of placeholder as I went about making points that didn't hinge on slight discrepancies among various commonly held definitions of the word, assuming the reader had a general sense of what I meant. In this chapter, I dwell on that one word and consider what it means to different people, what is at stake when we refer to a group as a community, and whether or not it's an appropriate designation for subreddits or Reddit as a whole.

There is a way in which academic arguments over the meanings of words can seem to move us further from a genuine understanding of things, leading us down long, narrow, hard-to-follow corridors of reasoning. And yet, the ability of words like "community" to affect how we understand Reddit is undeniable, though hard to recognize at first. The label or name of a thing has a way of determining how we think about it: our initial orientation toward it, our assumptions about how it works and what its potential might be, the types of questions we think to ask about it.

This is especially relevant to how we think about any new technological or social phenomenon. As we struggle to make sense of something new, we use language to put it into an existing category. The category may seem adequate at first but as time goes on and the new technology or phenomenon comes into its own, we sometimes see how inadequate the categorization has become. For example, referring to the small rectangular devices we carry around with us as "phones" (short for "telephones") has come to seem comically uninclusive of their uses.

But there are subtler, more complicated cases. Consider how the use of the word "friend" to refer to social media connections shaped our early orientations toward and assumptions about those technologies.

DOI: 10.4324/9781003150800-6

Such cases also have a way of prompting us to re-examine our assumptions not just about the new technology or phenomenon but also about the term itself. What is the difference between a friend and an acquaintance? Have the definitions of these words changed over time and across cultures? How might the addition of a few more categories of social connection influence our relationships as well as our thinking about them?

The word "community," like "democracy," has come to *represent* something: a vaguely defined unalloyed good, the civic counterpart to domestic "family." This positive association and semantic flexibility make the word a useful tool for anyone seeking to defend a group or a technology against criticism. It's easy to see the deployment of the word "community" as a strategic move on the part of social media moguls to shore up good will toward their products. However, the word has a longer history among those trying to make sense of group communication online. How else to refer to groups that looked and behaved, for all intents and purposes, like offline communities?

In this chapter, I delve into those first attempts to make sense of group communication online, and then go further back, to the last time our sense of what it means to be part of a non-familial group was profoundly disrupted. I then review empirical research on the social dynamics of Reddit in an attempt to determine whether or not it is appropriate to think of Reddit as either a community or as an ecosystem of smaller, discrete communities. I conclude by considering alternative designations for these groups.

What "community" meant

The question of whether or not particular online groups are communities was preceded by the question of whether it was even possible for community to exist online. The word "virtual" became an indispensable qualifier, allowing online groups to be referred to as communities while privileging offline communities as original, authentic, and "real" in a way that online communities, it was assumed, could never quite achieve. Anecdotes chronicling acts of sacrifice and social support among strangers[1] were used to make the case that online groups were as community-like as bowling leagues, church groups, and other beloved civic organizations (Rheingold, 1993). Despite an absence of the social cues and accountability that came with fixed identities and reputations, early online groups looked and behaved a lot like communities.

Such accounts often dwelled on the novel ways in which online communities transcended physical place (e.g., Castells, 1996). The ability to communicate instantaneously with others across great distances had existed during much of the 20th century, after the popularization of the telegraph and the telephone. Each of these technologies were seen as profoundly disruptive to the social order before becoming "domesticated" and integrated into everyday life (Marvin, 1988). They were also used primarily for one-to-one communication among individuals who had pre-established social connections to one another. Thus, their power to disrupt lay chiefly in their ability to affect interpersonal relationships rather than as a means of re-defining group identities. The internet had the potential to re-configure societies at an unprecedented scale.

Physical proximity was not the only factor shaping group identity prior to the 21st century. Social networks governed flows of commerce and information long before the rise of social media, but those networks were embedded in cultural contexts that were in large part constrained by geography. Mass media like newsprint, film, and radio transcended place and thus had the power to create new kinds of massive communities, forging new sets of shared values and history based on shared events, stories, and symbols (Anderson, 1983). These "imagined communities" stretched the definition of the word "community," involving minimal interaction among or knowledge of fellow community members. Nevertheless, bonds among members of imagined communities were undeniable; people were willing to die for a country composed of individuals whom they would never meet. Unsurprisingly, this ability to forge nationalist identities made mass media a convenient tool for authoritarian rulers who convinced citizens to do their bidding under the guise of selfless sacrifice for their fellow community members (Anderson, 1983).

Online communities promised to evolve in a less choreographed, more organic fashion. Instead of being defined by physical proximity or nationality, online communities would arise from shared sets of interests. In addition to sharing interests, members of online communities shared customs and practices as well as resources and support, forging a sense of group identity within a shared virtual space (Baym, 2015). As time went on and online group communication became more common and familiar, it became easier to argue that small, intimate circles of friends who regularly interacted online were as real as any other kind of community. But what about the loose groupings of "friends" on social media who seldom interacted, or the massive aggregations of followers and subscribers that felt strongly bonded to content creators but thought of their fellow fans as a sympathetic, undifferentiated mass? The question was no longer whether or not community *could* exist online, but rather *what types* of online group interaction were indicative of "true community."

Questions and concerns about community online echo those raised in the second half of the 19th century by another pervasive social phenomenon: the urbanization of industrialized societies. The field of sociology arose at a time when the rapid urbanization of Western Europe and the United States threatened to dissolve social bonds established in the villages, towns, and small cities of pre-19th-century society. The rapid shift in connections among individuals living in cities prompted fears of mass alienation, anomie, and hostility, and declining mental health (Simmel, 1903/1950). It also gave rise to a nostalgia for spontaneously occurring allegiances among individuals unrelated by blood and therefore absent of any obvious incentive to sacrifice for one another, bound by some invisible social contract.

Rapid urbanization threw the inner workings of traditional, smaller communities into relief. Now that sociologists had something to which they could compare true community, they could better articulate its essence. In looking back to the ideas of these scholars, we can find unexpected parallels not just between concerns about urbanization and "virtualization" of society, but also between the mechanisms of the city and the mechanisms of Reddit.

Applying Tönnies

It should come as no surprise that one of the first prominent critics of city life grew up on a prosperous farm. German sociologist Ferdinand Tönnies's early adulthood coincided with Europe's transition from a primarily agrarian economy to an industrial one. This, along with rising birth rates in Germany and much of Europe, led to the greatest migratory shift in human history: from countrysides to cities (Hochstadt, 1999). When we think of "modernization" of a society or "modernity" in general, we are contrasting a way of life that preceded this reorganization of communal life with the one that followed.

In his landmark work, *Community and Civil Society,* Tönnies labeled these ways of life and described what made them distinct from one another (1887/2001). "*Gemeinschaft*" was true community: something organic, an extension of the family based on deep mutual understanding. "*Gesellschaft*," by contrast, was modernized society: something designed, an imposition of the state that cultivated self-interest and alienation from one's fellow citizens. Isolating the precise qualities of cities that accounted for these differences necessitated identifying society's component parts, each of which has a counterpart in the online communities of Reddit.

One of Tönnies' key concepts is "*authority*": those who have power over others and the mechanisms used to legitimate or limit that power. Administrators are Reddit's ultimate authority – they can overrule moderators, ban users or entire subreddits, or change how part or all of the platform works (e.g., eliminating default subreddits). This power is kept in check by administrators' dependence on moderators to manage the millions of subreddits and make them more enjoyable and valuable for other users. Administrators also rely on contributors' labor (users finding noteworthy content online and posting it to Reddit), attention (users paying attention to advertisements), and capital (in the case of users who purchase Reddit Gold) to maintain the platform's monetary value. Similarly, moderators have the power to ban users and remove posts and comments, which is counterbalanced by users' willingness to contribute appealing content to the subreddit thereby making the subreddit a valued destination.

Are there individual Reddit users who are neither administrators nor moderators who have any degree of authority? Users with a lot of karma – so-called "power users" – may act as authorities in two ways. They may establish a "brand identity": their opinions and preferences garnering more attention than those of other users. But brand identity depends on recognizability, a quality that Reddit's identity minimalism makes difficult to cultivate. Within some subreddits, moderator-allocated flair can identify particular users as authorities, affording them some degree of deference or trust. Beyond this, power users may still have a kind of authority because they can drive the conversations on a given subreddit, or Reddit in general, in a particular direction by posting certain content. As in the cases of administrators and moderators, power users' authority is bounded by the collective will of other Reddit users in a way that is similar to the limits of the power of advertisers to alter consumer behavior or the ability of news sources to sway public opinion. Power users perform an agenda setting function (McCombs & Shaw, 1972), focusing users' attention on particular pieces of content without altering their fundamental orientations toward the content.

The unpaid, volunteer nature of the work that moderators and power users perform is significant. Tönnies makes the distinction between *Gemeinschaft* and *Gesellschaft* by noting that the latter replaced labor motivated by personal passion with labor motivated by

monetary compensation. Additionally, *Gesellschaft* replaces informal networks built on mutual trust with formal contracts, imposing economic and legal structures on personal relationships among citizens. It is easy to see parallels between *Gesellschaft* and the emergent public sphere online. Many popular social platforms like YouTube, Instagram, and TikTok have formalized the means by which users turn their relationships with other users into monetary profit. As of 2021, Reddit has eschewed this revenue model, maintaining at least one aspect of Tönnies's definition of true community.

But perhaps this is too narrow an interpretation of Tönnies's critique of the underlying forces that turn true community into something soulless and corrupt. Within the attention economy of Reddit, votes function as a kind of "currency," influencing behavior in much the same ways money influences it in other contexts. Karma, like money and like the number of subscribers and followers a user has on other platforms, quantifies and standardizes human desire, making it portable and stripping it of social context. Instead of focusing on connecting with others, contributors may – consciously or not – focus on impressing and entertaining others so as to acquire karma. In Reddit's *Gesellschaft*, genuine self-expression is replaced by the need to chase upvotes.

This isn't to say that communication in offline contexts is not influenced by the desire to impress and entertain others so as to burnish one's reputation. Too often, online social interaction is compared to an idealized offline version that either never existed, or if it did, was never the norm. It isn't hard for most of us to think of people we've met who attempt to turn social interactions into opportunities for personal gain, offline as well as online. Tönnies's insight was that the structure of the social environment can encourage or discourage pre-existing instincts toward self-interest.

Here, it is important to remember Reddit's modularity, and the extent to which its subreddits vary: in how they are governed, in topic, and in size. Might some intervention – hiding vote scores on comments and posts or changing the threshold needed to reach r/popular (or eliminating r/popular altogether) – mitigate status-seeking behavior, returning Reddit or a particular subreddit to a more neighborhood-like ideal? As Tönnies and other social theorists of the day would have it, such measures would largely be in vain. What mattered most was size. Even in the absence of top-down impositions of authority, the massification of individuals erodes close ties we associate with true community, imposing a kind of market logic on all expressions and interactions.

Here, it is worth considering the role of vote scores in large or small subreddits from the perspective of the browsing user. In a small subreddit, a browser can easily read all posts and comments posted in a given time period; votes have little function in terms of driving visibility. But at a certain point, the subreddit accrues so many posts, and the posts accrue so many comments, that reading all of the posts or comments becomes burdensome. Upvotes become a necessary way for the user to know what is of value, turning conversations into consumable content.

As valuable as established social theories like those of Tönnies are to understanding Reddit, it is important to compliment the perspectives they provide with a review of the empirical research on the social dynamics of Reddit. The following section moves us from abstract notions of community to concrete, observable characteristics of it.

Empirical investigations of community on Reddit

There is, of course, no magic formula for determining a group's "community-ness." One approach is to talk to members of the group and ask them whether or not they feel a sense of community. In interviews, contributors to subreddits are apt to casually refer to themselves and their fellow contributors as "we," which suggests feelings of affiliation and belonging (Fernback, 2007; Kiene, Monroy-Hernandez, & Hill, 2016; Massanari, 2015). In a survey study, Howard and Magee (2013) provided evidence that a subset of Reddit users identify strongly with other Reddit users as a group, expressing feelings of solidarity and commitment toward the group. These definitions and measures really measure *perceptions of group identity*, which leaves room for groups in which individuals never interact with fellow members, something more akin to an online version of Anderson's imagined communities (Gruzd, Wellman, & Takhteyev, 2011).

Members of "communities of affiliation" like a nation or even a racial or gender identity category may experience strong feelings of belonging, solidarity, and commitment, but they do not necessarily interact with one another or know one another as individuals. By contrast, other communities demand, or at least expect, some level of interaction among all or most of their members. Interaction does not, by itself, create community. Crowds that rapidly form and disperse are rarely regarded as communities, even if crowd members interact with one another. We might refer to groups in which there is *prolonged interaction* among members as "participatory communities." Most accounts of online community – whether extolling their virtues (e.g., Armstrong & Hagel, 2000) or demonstrating the threat some of them pose (e.g., Sowles et al., 2018; Subtirelu, 2017) – tend to conceive of online community as participatory. This isn't surprising given that one of the defining features of the popularized internet was that it allowed for mass interaction among users.

This definition of community is one that lends itself to research through observation. Digital interactions leave observable traces – archived conversations, hyperlinks, metadata – providing scholars who study online communities with a powerful new tool for understanding how they function (Golder & Macy, 2014; Watts, 2011). There are many studies of subreddit communities that analyze the content of posts and comments, each of which sheds light on how communities on Reddit function (e.g., Bhandari & Armstrong, 2019; Cunha et al., 2016; Gray & Kou, 2019; Park & Conway, 2017; McEwan, 2016). They do not, for the most part, consider the size of the participatory communities within the large groups of visitors who do not contribute to discourse.

Continuous, active participation in a group has been used by multiple internet researchers as a way to define community membership online (Panek et al., 2018; Preece, 2000; Ridings, Gefen, & Arinze, 2002). Over the past several years, our research team has sought to determine the number of users who actively participate in Reddit's discourse and to determine whether these users continue to contribute over time. Consistent with observations of other online platforms on which participation is possible such as Digg.com (Lerman, 2007), Wikipedia (Ortega, Gonzalez-Barahona, & Robles, 2008), and Yahoo! Answers (Shah, Oh, & Oh, 2008), we found that very few subscribers to subreddits actively participate in them.

As subreddits grow, the percentage of subscribers who actively participate tends to shrink. In the larger subreddits, participation rates among subscribers tended to peak between 5% and 10% in their early stages of development, decreasing to between one percent and a tenth of a percent when the subreddit expanded to its largest observed size. The number of commenters tends to increase as the number of subscribers increases, but they increase at different rates. A greater proportion of the early subscribers to the subreddit tend to actively participate in its discourse relative to later subscribers. There can be surges of new commenters when an event happens – a video game is released, or a news event or championship occurs – but generally, the pattern of early, more active adopters holds across subreddits.

Different types of subreddits tend to correspond to different participation rates. Smaller Appreciation, Affinity, and Fandom (AAF) subreddits tend to have higher participation rates (18% for r/FireEmblemHeroes in November of 2017) than Spectacle subreddits (3% for r/

AnimalsBeingBros in April 2014). Educational subreddits tend to be somewhere in the middle (r/Arduino, a subreddit dedicated to discussions of the open source technology Arduino, fluctuated between 7% and 2%).

Political movement subreddits tend to be more active, particularly during the initial phase of excitement over a candidate. As then-US-presidential-candidate Donald Trump gained momentum in April of 2016, roughly 62% of r/The_Donald's 90,000 subscribers commented on the subreddit; by early 2019, after Trump had been elected President, 7% of subscribers were commenting. In mid-2015, 20% of SandersForPresident's 62,000 subscribers were commenting, rising to 32% by March 2016 before dipping to 13% by July of 2016.

As noted in Chapter 2, r/AskReddit is an outlier in terms of its number of comments, and this is also true of the number of commenters. Whereas most of the largest subreddits would have between 100,000 and 200,000 commenters per month, r/AskReddit has regularly exceeded 500,000 commenters per month after 2016.

This analysis gives us some idea of how many subscribers to subreddits are active participants, but does not differentiate between contributors who comment only once or twice and contributors who dominate the discourse, commenting hundreds of times to a subreddit. To evaluate the extent to which participation was evenly distributed among those who chose to comment, our research team used a statistic commonly used in economics to evaluate distribution of wealth: the Gini coefficient (Panek et al., 2018). The Gini coefficient fluctuates between 0 and 1. If all comments in a given subreddit were posted by a single contributor, the Gini coefficient would equal to 1, and if every user who commented contributed an equal number of comments, the Gini coefficient would be equal to 0.

Figure 6.1 illustrates how the Gini coefficient corresponds to different distributions of comments among commenters to a subreddit. The figure depicts comment distribution during April 2015 in three subreddits: r/IAmA, r/TwoXChromosomes, and r/CFB. As noted in the chart's key on the right side of the figure, the Gini coefficients of these three subreddits vary between .43 and .73. Along the X axis, commenters are divided into 10 percentiles based on the frequency with which they commented – the contributors who commented the most frequently to the subreddit are in the 1st percentile while the contributors who commented the least frequently are in the 10th percentile. In the subreddit with the highest Gini coefficient (r/CFB), the 1st percentile accounts for a larger proportion of the comments (69%) than is the case in the other subreddits (57% for x/TwoXChromosomes and 44% for r/IAmA).

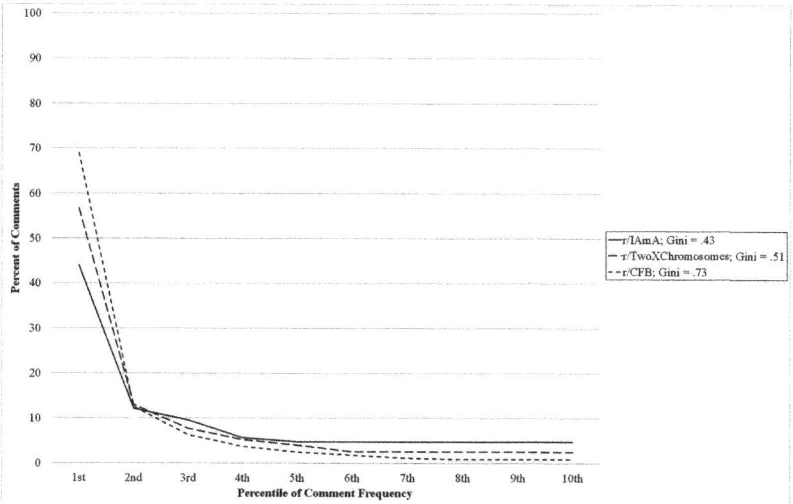

Figure 6.1 Comment distributions across contributors to r/IAmA, r/TwoXChromosomes, and r/CFB in April 2015.

Generally, subreddits' Gini coefficients tend to be between .4 and .8, with the majority of contributors commenting no more than a few comments per month and 10% of contributors accounting for between one-half and two-thirds of comments in a given month. This is the case for a wide variety of subreddit types and sizes. The general trend is for subreddits to start with participation more widely distributed among contributors, and then to become dominated by a smaller percentage of contributors as it grows.

Another trend emerging from our exploratory analyses is that Public Sphere subreddits like r/news, r/worldnews, and r/politics tend to have higher Gini coefficients (typically between .6 to .8) than those observed in most other subreddits. This means that fewer people account for more comments than in other subreddits. Subreddits that represent clear ideological agendas (r/TheRedPill, r/FatPeopleHate, r/The_Donald) tend to have higher Gini coefficients as well. This has significant implications for our understanding of the online public sphere. Not only do very few Reddit users comment in subreddits relating to public affairs. Of those who comment, discourse tends to be more unevenly distributed than is generally the case on Reddit.

When we explored the distribution of vote scores[2] across authors, we found votes to be even more highly concentrated than the proportion of comments in a given month. Typically, the top 10% of contributors' comments garnered between 70% and 85% of the total vote scores for comments in a subreddit in a given month. This pattern appeared to hold true across different types of subreddits.

We also examined how many commenters returned to the subreddit to comment again. We looked at this in two ways: tracking subreddit commenter retention month-to-month and tracking subreddit commenter "cohorts" over time. Findings from both analyses were similar to what we found regarding participation rates. By the time subreddits reached 5,000 commenters, at least two-thirds of the first-time commenters would not return in the next month. A year after they had first commented, roughly 85%–95% of those commenters had stopped commenting. This left a "loyal core" of commenters that could be as large as 4,000 commenters (roughly 15% of the contributors who first commented in r/Politics in February of 2016).

In Song's (2009) terms, most subreddits are highly "porous," with commenters coming and going with great frequency. Each subreddit we examined had a loyal core of contributors to discourse, but they represented a fraction of the users who contributed to discourse in a given time period. We should not, however, jump to the conclusion that Reddit as a whole is highly porous. Examining the commenting and posting behavior of over 7 million Reddit users, Valensise and colleagues (2019) find that contributors often fluctuate among different subreddits over time, remaining active members of the larger group of Reddit contributors while participating in particular subreddits' discourse only intermittently.

A contributor might not even recognize that they are "in" a particular subreddit when they comment, having clicked on a post in their feed and read the post without looking at the name of the subreddit. Subreddit designations, like usernames, are not prominently featured and are thus possible to overlook. There are likely some commenters who go straight to subreddits and dwell in them before posting or commenting, while others may flit from subreddit to subreddit with minimal awareness of the distinction among them.

The design of Reddit may make subreddits appear more discreet than they are in practice. Unlike other popular social platforms like YouTube and Twitter, Reddit features destinations for particular interest communities to congregate. But design should not be confused with patterns of actual use, the latter of which suggest something other than our accepted definition of "true community." Given these observations, it is worth considering whether "community" is the most accurate word to describe group activity on Reddit. We now consider two alternative designations for this activity.

Community, network or feed?

Many of the most widely used theories and methods for investigating group behavior online focus on networks. This framework is a natural fit for describing two of the most important aspects of the internet during the first decade of the 21st century: the linkages among websites on which Google based its original search algorithm, and the linkages among users of popular Social Networking Sites (SNSs) such as Friendster, MySpace, and Facebook. Users of SNSs are linked to other users through observable, measurable actions: friending, following, liking, replying to or commenting on, sharing, retweeting. Each action can be understood as a tie between nodes on a network, each of which is strengthened upon repetition.

For the most part, Reddit users are not linked together in these ways. Though Reddit eventually allowed users to follow other users,[3] for most of its first 15 years, users subscribed to subreddits rather than to individual users. Reddit contributors reply to one another, but the de-emphasis on individual identity and the size of many subreddits make it unlikely that these connections are as reciprocal as they would be on social platforms (Lewis, 2015). Voting is a kind of tie between users, but voting is done anonymously on Reddit. Voting networks might be of interest to the researcher, but not to the user, who cannot use the information of who downvoted or upvoted their post or comment in any way.

Just because users do not experience Reddit as a network does not mean that their interactions with other users and content might not be elucidated by social network analysis and theory. Mapping the webs of second or third-degree connections among users or subreddits may tell us something about group behavior on Reddit, even if this behavior is much more diffuse than what we typically regard as a community. Taking stock of online group communication in the early 21st century, Rainie and Wellman (2012) coined the term "networked individualism." The online groups that they observed were looser, more fragmented, and typically larger and more diverse than offline groups such as church groups or neighborhood associations. They tended to coalesce quickly in times of crisis or triumph, only to disperse just as quickly, and in many cases, never reform in precisely the same configuration again.

Online groups may be located along a continuum, ranging from tighter, cohesive networks to looser, more porous ones. A small group of individuals who meet online regularly to play a video game are smaller, tighter, and less fragmented. Millions of Twitter or YouTube users who, in one way or another, interact with one another are much larger, looser, more fragmentary networks. Based on our research team's observations, most subreddits are toward the latter end of the spectrum: there is little regularity to their interactions, they are often large in size, and members come and go frequently. Subreddits possess small cores and large peripheries (see Figure 6.2 for an example).

As Rainie and Wellman note (2012), the size of loose networks is one reason they are able to sustain themselves over time despite rapid turnover. Larger size compensates for the lack of effortful coordination among members to formally delegate duties or communicate at appointed times. An individual may post a question to a subreddit, or may go to a subreddit seeking mere distraction. If the subreddit is too small, the user may have to wait a long time for the desired content to appear. But if the subreddit is sufficiently large, the odds are greater than at any given moment, one contributor will provide the desired content.

Network analysis is also useful for mapping flows of attention, particularly whether each node is just as apt to receive attention as it is to pay it to others. In this sense, Reddit is a highly asymmetric

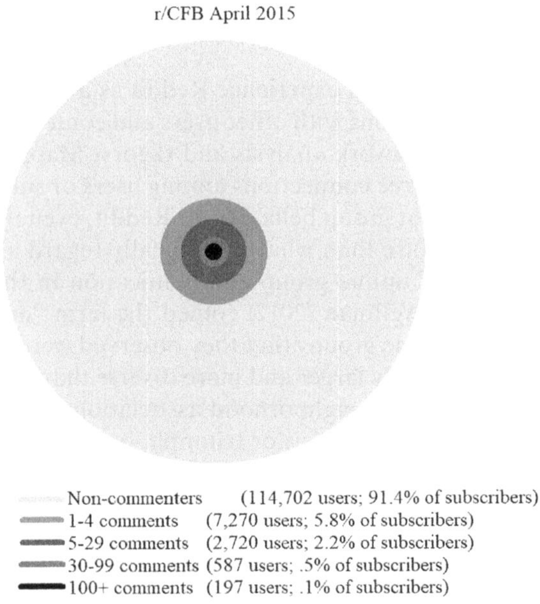

Figure 6.2 Subscribers and commenters to r/CFB in April 2015.

network, with attention flowing from the majority of its users toward the content and comments posted by a much smaller number of contributors. The majority of Reddit users experience it not as a community nor as a network, but as a content feed, albeit one composed of user-generated or user-curated content. The feed can be customized, as when registered users subscribe to particular subreddits, or generic, as in the case of r/all and r/popular. Common to many popular social media platforms of the 21st century, the feed is often regarded as a culturally debased form, associated with addictive, habitual scrolling and the eradication of important, meaningful context. Whereas the community is the building block of civilization and the network is its underlying structure, the feed is seen as a mindless, endless distraction.

Conclusion

Perhaps the large, porous, fleeting congregations of Reddit are not as novel as they initially seem. In their assessment of early online communities, Wellman and Gulia (1999) argue that this way of encountering communities – fleetingly, intermittently – is, for the most part, common to modern societies. Most citizens of post-industrialized societies, when in need of support or resources, do not go to a single group for all their social, spiritual, and material needs. Instead, they draw from "differentiated portfolios" of social connections (p. 171), accessing different clusters of individuals at different times based on changing needs and desires. This is not to say that Reddit users' fickleness is not different from the face-to-face social activities of the average citizen in modern society, but that it is perhaps best to think of such differences as ones of degree rather than kind. Just as contemporary historical research on much-revered 18th-century coffee houses revealed them to be less egalitarian and erudite than was often assumed (Ellis, 2017), such a perspective on modern face-to-face communities serves as a reminder not to succumb to the temptation of comparing unfavorably the communities of Reddit to perfectly cohesive, discrete, face-to-face communities.

As with other popular social media platforms (e.g., YouTube), Reddit is a venue where the sets of interactions and feelings that are most commonly associated with "community" are possible, but not inevitable, nor especially likely or common. Just as YouTube is commonly used as a source of on-demand instructional, educational, or entertainment video content, Reddit is often used simply as a crowdsourced content sorter.

Perhaps there is a limit to the light that can be shed by comparing Reddit to other types of groups. Maybe we need a new name for what we see on Reddit: relatively small groups engaging in what early internet scholars and many sociologists would consider "community" while a much larger group watches, votes, and, occasionally, chimes in (what we might call "chimers," as distinct from visitors or lurkers who never contribute to content or discourse). As with words like "friend," "follower," "like," and "share," the word "community," as it pertains to group activity on Reddit, is a kind of skeuomorph – retaining the basic features of the original while evolving into something new.

Notes

1 Just as the increasing prevalence of online relationships caused us to reconsider what we meant when we called someone a friend, it is continuing to cause us to reconsider the designation of "stranger."
2 Vote scores are determined by subtracting the total number of downvotes a comment receives from the total number of upvotes it receives.
3 https://www.reddit.com/r/announcements/comments/60p3n1/tldr_today_were_testing_out_a_new_feature_that/

References

Anderson, B. (1983). *Imagined communities: Reflections on the origin and spread of nationalism*. London: Verso.
Armstrong, A., & Hagel, J. (2000). The real value of online communities. In E. Lesser, M. Fontaine, & J. Slusher (Eds.) *Knowledge and communities* (pp. 85–95). London: Routledge.
Baym, N. K. (2015). *Personal connections in the digital age*. Cambridge, MA: Polity Press.
Bhandari, A., & Armstrong, C. (2019, November). Tkol, httt, and r/radiohead: High affinity terms in Reddit communities. In *Proceedings of the 5th workshop on noisy user-generated text (W-NUT 2019)* (pp. 57–67). Hong Kong: Xu, Ritter, Baldwin, & Rahimi.
Castells, M. (1996). *The rise of the network society, the information age: Economy, society and culture Vol. I*. Oxford: Blackwell.
Cunha, T. O., Weber, I., Haddadi, H., & Pappa, G. L. (2016, April). The effect of social feedback in a reddit weight loss community. In *Proceedings of the 6th international conference on digital health conference* (pp. 99–103). Montreal, Quebec: Association for Computer Machinery.
Ellis, M. (2017). *Eighteenth-century coffee-house culture: Restoration satire*. New York: Routledge.
Fernback, J. (2007). Beyond the diluted community concept: A symbolic interactionist perspective on online social relations. *New Media & Society*, *9*(1), 49–69.

Golder, S. A., & Macy, M. W. (2014). Digital footprints: Opportunities and challenges for online social research. *Annual Review of Sociology, 40*, 129–152.

Gray, C. M., & Kou, Y. (2019). Co-producing, curating, and defining design knowledge in an online practitioner community. *CoDesign, 15*(1), 41–58.

Gruzd, A., Wellman, B., & Takhteyev, Y. (2011). Imagining Twitter as an imagined community. *American Behavioral Scientist, 55*(10), 1294–1318.

Hochstadt, S. (1999). *Mobility and modernity: Migration in Germany, 1820–1989*. Ann Arbor: University of Michigan Press.

Howard, M. C., & Magee, S. M. (2013). To boldly go where no group has gone before: An analysis of online group identity and validation of a measure. *Computers in Human Behavior, 29*(5), 2058–2071.

Kiene, C., Monroy-Hernández, A., & Hill, B. M. (2016, May). Surviving an "Eternal September": How an online community managed a surge of newcomers. In *Proceedings of the 2016 CHI conference on human factors in computing systems* (pp. 1152–1156). San Jose, CA: Association of Computing Machinery.

Lerman, K. (2007). User participation in social media: Digg study. In *Proceedings of the 2007 IEEE/WIC/ACM international conferences on web intelligence and intelligent agent technology-workshops* (pp. 255–258). Los Alamitos, CA: IEEE Computer Society.

Lewis, S. C. (2015). Reciprocity as a key concept for social media and society. *Social Media + Society, 1*(1), 1–2.

Marvin, C. (1988). *When old technologies were new: Thinking about electric communication in the late nineteenth century*. Oxford: Oxford University Press.

Massanari, A. (2015). *Participatory culture, community, and play: Learning from Reddit*. New York: Peter Lang.

McCombs, M. E., & Shaw, D. L. (1972). The agenda-setting function of mass media. *Public Opinion Quarterly, 36*(2), 176–187.

McEwan, B. (2016). Communication of communities: Linguistic signals of online groups. *Information, Communication & Society, 19*(9), 1233–1249.

Ortega, F., Gonzalez-Barahona, J. M., & Robles, G. (2008). On the inequality of contributions to Wikipedia. In *Proceedings of the 41st annual Hawaii international conference on system sciences* (pp. 304–304). Piscataway, NJ: IEEE Press.

Panek, E., Hollenbach, C., Yang, J., & Rhodes, T. (2018). The effects of group size and time on the formation of online communities: Evidence from reddit. *Social Media + Society, 4*(4), 2056305118815908.

Park, A., & Conway, M. (2017). Tracking health related discussions on Reddit for public health applications. In *AMIA annual symposium proceedings* (Vol. 2017, p. 1362). American Medical Informatics Association: Washington, DC.

Preece, J. (2000). *Online communities: Designing usability, supporting sociability*. Chichester: John Wiley & Sons.

Rainie, H., & Wellman, B. (2012). *Networked: The new social operating system*. Cambridge, MA: MIT Press.

Rheingold, H. (1993). *The virtual community: Homesteading on the electronic frontier*. Reading, MA: Addison-Wesley Publishing.

Ridings, C. M., Gefen, D., & Arinze, B. (2002). Some antecedents and effects of trust in virtual communities. *The Journal of Strategic Information Systems, 11*(3–4), 271–295.

Shah, C., Oh, J. S., & Oh, S. (2008). Exploring characteristics and effects of user participation in online social Q&A sites. *First Monday, 13*(9).

Simmel, G. (1903/1950). The metropolis and mental life. In K. H. Wolff (Ed.) *The Sociology of Georg Simmel* (pp. 409–424). New York: The Free Press.

Sowles, S. J., McLeary, M., Optican, A., Cahn, E., Krauss, M. J., Fitzsimmons-Craft, E. E., Wilfley, D. E., & Cavazos-Rehg, P. A. (2018). A content analysis of an online pro-eating disorder community on Reddit. *Body Image, 24,* 137–144.

Subtirelu, N. C. (2017). Donald Trump supporters and the denial of racism: An analysis of online discourse in a pro-Trump community. *Journal of Language Aggression and Conflict*, *5*(2), 323–346.

Tönnies, F., Geuss, R., Hollis, M., & Skinner, Q. (1887/2001). *Tönnies: Community and civil society*. Cambridge: Cambridge University Press.

Valensise, C. M., Cinelli, M., Galeazzi, A., & Quattrociocchi, W. (2019). Drifts and shifts: Characterizing the evolution of users interests on Reddit. *arXiv preprint* arXiv:1912.09210.

Watts, D. J. (2011). *Everything Is obvious: How common sense fails us*. New York: Crown Business.

Wellman, B., & Gulia, M. (1999). Virtual communities as communities. In M. A. Smith & P. Kullock (Eds.) *Communities in cyberspace* (pp. 167–194). London: Routledge.

7 Reddit and journalism

r/nytimes was among the first subreddits to be created by Reddit's administrators, before users had the ability to create their own subreddits. It was established as a functional equivalent of an RSS feed: a way for *The New York Times* to auto-publish links to its stories on another platform. In its first year, the number of posts on r/nytimes increased from 60 per month to 300, but the posts were not garnering engagement in the form of either votes or comments. By 2008, two years after its creation, the subreddit was moribund, containing a few stray posts from interloping spammers. Years later, after *The New York Times* put most of its content behind a paywall, the subreddit was commandeered by a user who programmed a bot to continually post links to *New York Times* stories as a way to provide other Reddit users' free access to them.

The New York Times's initial approach toward Reddit tells us something about how the field of journalism viewed Reddit during the platform's early years. First, it suggests that established news companies took Reddit seriously enough to try to reach an audience through it. Second, it reflects an earlier era in which news from particular sources lived in certain identifiable destinations: cable channels, websites such as CNN.com, and – perhaps – dedicated subreddits. Users sought out news, so the thinking went, based on their preferences for identifiable and trusted news brands.

Reddit's rise coincided with radical transformations of news consumption patterns and the print journalism industry. These processes were well underway before Reddit reached enough people to be considered influential, so it is difficult to cast the platform as the first and only reason for the disruption and easier to see it as part of a trend. The transformation has been referred to as a "death" by some (e.g., McChesney & Nichols, 2011) but it is clear that as of the writing of this book, news consumption has not died.

DOI: 10.4324/9781003150800-7

The business of journalism is another matter, which is more easily characterized as "in crisis" if not quite dead (Abramson, 2019; Grieco, 2020). The primary medium through which news was consumed for centuries – the newspaper – has become a kind of atrophied organ or relic from another time. As inert and antiquated as they may seem, newspapers are worth considering when attempting to understand Reddit as a news source. Newspapers' formatting and function, along with those of magazines and newsletters, suggest a kinship with Reddit: both are aggregations of items that are mostly about current events, displayed in easily scannable printed words and still images, made available and of interest to the general public.

If Reddit didn't start the fire that burned down the news business and altered – if not eliminated – news consumption habits, where does it fit into the story? In this chapter, I will discuss Reddit and journalism primarily from a content and consumption perspective, focusing on Reddit's role in the transformation of news in the first and second decades of the 21st century.

A brief history of online news

As with democracy and community, digital disruption has inspired us to ask about the original meaning of the word "news." What is the point of news? Is it merely to supply relevant, accurate information about current events? Is it required to offer analysis of those events? Is it intended to inspire conversation and debate? If these functions were all bundled together in the popular newspapers of the 20th century, have Reddit and other popular "social news" platforms led to their unbundling?

The existence of news as information that is of *general* interest – as opposed to topics of interest to a select (often physically proximate) few – should not be taken for granted. For most of human history, most people lived in what we would now regard as a fragmented information environment, only vaguely aware of or interested in current events outside of their limited social circles. The advent of the newspaper helped create a general public, though at first, limits on access, literacy, and interest kept this group from growing very large (Starr, 2004). It was not until the widespread popularization of newspapers along with popular radio and television news of the mid-20th century that a broad news-consuming public came into existence. This is a useful context to keep in mind when considering one of the oft-mentioned facets of the journalism crisis of the early 21st century: audience fragmentation. Historically speaking, large groups of people unified by a singular information environment is an anomaly.

Broadcast radio and television news supplemented newsprint in the media marketplace rather than replacing it. Why, then, has the rise of news online come at the expense of print journalism? In the first phase of internet popularization (2000–2004), many legacy print news sources like *The New York Times, The Washington Post*, and local newspapers created websites that were essentially online versions of their print copies. Crucially, most legacy news companies offered these online versions for free, establishing the expectation among news consumers that news could be obtained for free online.

These sites faced competition from digital-native news blogs that took advantage of the speed, interactivity, and low overhead costs offered by web-only publishing. The writers and editors of blogs like *The Huffington Post* and *The Drudge Report* understood that traffic on the web was, at the time, driven by Google searches for stories, and that by optimizing their content (in particular, their headlines) for searches, they could reach larger audiences (Abramson, 2019). Blogs also understood that there were no rules or conventions regarding intellectual property online, which allowed them to repackage stories originally reported by established news sources and pass them off as their own content.

Their small size and willingness to break with traditional journalistic norms allowed blogs to be more nimble, adjusting to emerging trends in information technology and popular culture. Unburdened by the need to protect a long-established reputation, they could cater to the desires of office workers in need of brief distractions. Commentary and opinion pieces were less expensive to produce than original reportage, and so blogs' content tended to be more opinionated, more politically partisan, and more likely to exploit readers' bias toward information that confirmed their existing beliefs.

As Facebook and Twitter became increasingly popular ways for internet users to share news stories with one another, websites like Buzzfeed and Upworthy optimized their news content for sharing via social media rather than searching. The goals of popular websites shifted from trying to anticipate curiosity articulated through popular search phrases to causing social media users to share links to their stories, turning those users into de facto news content distributors. Key to Buzzfeed's initial approach was its ability to identify emerging topics that were gaining traction among a small, influential group of opinion leaders and repackage them for a broader audience. By measuring quantifiable social metrics of clicks, likes, and shares to discern these topics, Buzzfeed could determine which topics to cover in order to generate content that resonated with internet users. Twitter's growth in popularity during this time period provided an ideal source of publicly visible, quantified "buzz" to measure.

In many ways, this was not very different from what Reddit sought to do as it entered the online news distribution marketplace in the mid-2000s. Both Buzzfeed and Reddit were content-agnostic platforms that aggregated noteworthy content, inferring "noteworthiness" based on low-effort user metrics. Despite these similarities in origin of purpose, the platforms evolved in radically different ways, in large part because of the different design cultures from which they arose. Reddit arose from programmer/hacker culture of the late 20th century (see Chapter 3), while Buzzfeed came from a culture of journalism and Leftist politics. Both platforms claimed to reflect the desires and interests of online culture, but they derived these desires from different slices of the internet, leading to different emphases in their content. Buzzfeed's writers and editors re-packaged news of the day in a format conducive to virality while Reddit served as a venue in which news was re-distributed "as is" by its contributors. The topics, perspectives, and informality reflected in this content were arguably more representative of the general public than those embedded in news generated by legacy media companies, but were still based on the preferences of relatively small, non-representative samples of that public.

Much of the content circulated by Buzzfeed and its brethren was not easily characterized as "news." Lists of disgusting foods and images of cute animals seem more analogous to content found in leisure magazines, not *The New York Times*. And yet established news companies found themselves competing for attention with sites like Buzzfeed (Abramson, 2019), forcing them to adopt some of the techniques used by the upstart competition. Currentness and novelty were always central to the appeal of news, perhaps more than the high-minded ideal of creating an informed citizenry. Sites like Buzzfeed simply stripped away the imposed ideals and standards of news editors, leaving only content that satisfies the desire for something new and interesting.

Aggregation and disaggregation

Buzzfeed and Reddit aggregated stories from a variety of news sources, and could thus be referred to as "news aggregators." At the same time, they took stories out of the original contexts in which they were published, *disaggregating* a structured, semi-cohesive text – the daily newspaper – into discreet articles, some of which were of more interest to the platforms' users than others. Furthermore, Reddit's design separates the title of the post from the content to which it refers; Reddit users see lists of titles and must click on the titles in order to read more. In the case of links to news stories, post titles – either copied verbatim from the news source or re-written to garner more attention on Reddit – act as headlines, conveying the essence of the story. But whereas physical newspapers and digital news websites paired headlines and stories with one another in a seamless visual flow, Reddit's design disaggregated headlines from stories. Reddit's seamless visual flow was comprised only of headlines.

It was the linked headline, not the article itself nor the news source's reputation, that drove traffic to news websites. Instead of deriving revenue from subscriptions to an entire news site, legacy news sources derived it from exposure to advertising, and exposure varied greatly from article to article depending on how appealing its headline was to the "citizen editors" of platforms like Reddit. If one headline drives traffic to a news website far more than the others, the writer of that headline, it would stand to reason, would be rewarded and emulated. The difference in readership numbers between headlines that gain traction on social platforms and those that do not grows as platforms like Reddit and Twitter become more popular. This trend leads to a winner-take-all competition, increasing the incentive for reporters and editors to generate news with easily digestible, attention-grabbing headlines.

But how many Reddit users actually click on the linked headlines that appear on the site? It is easy enough for users to simply read the headline, vote, and comment without ever having followed the link, much less read the entirety of the news story. Here, we must remember that even in the heyday of newsprint, news consumers were headline-readers more than they were story-readers (Dor, 2003; Holmqvist et al., 2003; Nir, 1993; Schramm, 1947). As newspapers created digital versions of their print editions, researchers assessed the extent to which doing so decreased the likelihood that readers would actually read the stories (Holmqvist et al., 2003; Tewksbury & Althaus, 2000). They found that readers of digital editions scanned more and read less than readers of print editions. If Reddit's design has encouraged more headline-scanning and less-article reading, it has exacerbated an existing trend.

Another trend in online news that further contributed to the disaggregation of headlines from stories was legacy news sources' use of paywalls. In response to dramatic revenue losses during the first decade of the 21st century, companies such as *The New York Times* and *The Washington Post* erected paywalls that allowed non-paying users access to headlines and brief summaries but required them to pay either for the individual article or for a subscription in order to read the accompanying article. This tacit acknowledgement by news organizations that headlines have no monetary value online, that they are primarily a means of attracting customers to the true substance of news – the article – is significant in an information environment highly dependent on those headlines.

Consider the value of a headline from the perspective of Reddit's owners and administrators. Headlines generated by news organizations and posted by Reddit's contributors have always been a large part of what makes the site an attractive destination. Not only do these headlines serve users' desires for novel, noteworthy content; they also serve as a generator of conversation. The free circulation of headlines allowed Reddit to create and sustain a platform without having to pay for content.

The partial replacement of professional news editors with the citizen editors on Reddit and Twitter raises the question of whether reporters might be similarly replaced. If news headlines were what made these platforms valuable to their users, might they be able to cut out the middlepeople and generate their own news headlines?

Prior to the rise of blogs, Twitter, and the online participatory culture commonly referred to as *Web 2.0*, news reporters were the only means by which an individual in any given part of the world could know what was going on in any other part of it. Masspersonal media technologies gave individuals the power to broadcast to anyone else on the network, allowing any user to act as an on-the-scene reporter, albeit only in the most basic sense of the word (O'Sullivan & Carr, 2018). Citizen journalists were not trained to provide context, but the attention marketplace of the 21st century did not require them to be trained in this way. For a time, legacy organizations such as CNN used their established place in the news landscape to provide a venue for the work of citizen journalists to reach larger audiences, continuing to do so in a limited capacity (Allan & Thorson, 2009). Reddit gave citizen journalists the ability to bypass mainstream outlets and reach large audiences directly.

This mode of journalism was better suited to some current events than to others. When the facts of events were reasonably straightforward and publicly visible, legacy news resources were not needed to produce useful headlines. But when special access or knowledge was required in order to make sense of the event, citizen journalists were less well suited to the task of reportage. What's more, legacy news sources possessed reputations and were thus capable of being held accountable for untruths. Even when anyone with a smartphone can report an event, news organizations serve as brand names that news consumers can use to verify the veracity of such reports. The work of building up these reputations, of engaging in the unglamorous work of verification, are part of the oft-overlooked value of headlines generated by legacy news sources.

What we are left with is an information environment in which free headlines reach large audiences, perhaps larger than the readerships of newspapers or the viewerships of television news programming ever were. Platforms like Reddit that mix news content with other types of content complicate measuring exposure to news (Barthel et al., 2020), making it difficult to determine precisely how many users are exposed to news on Reddit. The number of subscribers to news subreddits (e.g., 26.5 million for r/worldnews as of July 2021) gives us some idea of news audience size on Reddit, but does not take into account visitors who are not logged in to Reddit or those who visit r/all and r/popular, both of which frequently feature posts from r/news, r/politics, and other news-related subreddits.

News on Reddit is not relegated to subreddits specifically designated for the purpose of sharing and discussing news. Many popular topic-specific subreddits (e.g., r/movies, r/sports, r/games) intermittently function as places to share and discuss news relating to that topic. Political subreddits such as r/politics, r/Conservative, or r/SandersForPresident function primarily as places to share political news. Strict definitions of news also exclude cases in which news topics spill over into broader discourse. Media scholars have for some time acknowledged the blurry lines between news and entertainment (e.g., Thussu, 2007; Tuchman, 1978) as well as the ways in which those seeking entertainment or distraction are "incidentally exposed" to news (Tewksbury, Weaver, & Maddex, 2001). Popular humor subreddits (e.g., r/dankmemes) and general purpose subreddits (e.g., r/pics) frequently feature posts that relate to current events and could thus be considered news sources in much the same way sitcom episodes or late-night talk show monologues relating to current events could be considered news sources (Moy, Xenos, & Hess, 2005).

Reading the comments

Beyond the basic function of informing citizens about current events, news serves as a catalyst for discussion, as "something to talk about." Commentary and discussion make up a significant portion of content on cable news networks and news radio programs, an unsurprising fact given the amount of time such networks and programs must fill as well as the cheap cost of producing commentary relative to the cost of reportage. Online, discussions of news, particularly political news, have flourished, expanding publicly visible news discussion beyond a small circle of pundits and media personalities.

This collective curation, evaluation, and discussion of news – what Alex Bruns (2005) refers to as "gatewatching" – has been an important part of the platform since Reddit's first post.[1] Reddit comments on news stories contain concise expressions of political belief, extended critiques, and links to other relevant news stories or information online. A decade-and-a-half into Reddit's existence, popular news subreddits such as r/news and r/worldnews have the highest comment-to-subscriber ratio among large subreddits,[2] suggesting that discussions of news continue to be central to the platform's appeal to users.

The nature of these news discussions on Reddit – their levels of civility, substance, and the extent to which users attempt to persuade others – varies depending on the extent to which the subreddit is ideologically homogeneous or heterogeneous (An et al., 2019; Duguay, 2021). Here again, the modular nature of Reddit creates opportunities for both kinds of communication spaces to arise. Whereas the kinds of cross-cutting exposure and engagement that is in evidence on undifferentiated public forums like Twitter and news website comment sections exist in larger subreddits like r/news, smaller ideologically homogeneous subreddits such as r/The_Donald feature less debate among contributors (An et al., 2019; Eady et al., 2019; Marchal, 2020).

Not all visitors to Reddit or news subreddits participate in these discussions. As noted in Chapters 5 and 6, a relatively small number of contributors account for a large number of comments on Reddit. It thus would be fruitful to conceptualize news discussions on Reddit as content in and of itself – created by a small number of contributors, consumed by a larger group of news consumers. The mere presence of comments on news websites can affect readers' perceptions of the article (Lee, 2012), which would lead us to expect a difference between the experiences of Reddit users who merely read post titles or linked-to news articles and those who read the comments.

What news sites does Reddit link to?

Regardless of whether or not Reddit users actually click on links to news articles, it is important to know what news sources make up Reddit's news landscape. A 2017 analysis of outgoing links to news websites showed that *The Guardian* and *The Independent* – two British news sources with large, global readerships – are the most linked-to news sources on Reddit's popular news subreddits (Hoffa, 2017). Both sources offer articles for free, in contrast to subscription-only legacy news sources such as *The New York Times* and *The Washington Post*, which have a markedly smaller presence on the platform. *The Hill* and *Politico,* two digital-native news sites dedicated to coverage of American political news, are frequently linked to from political subreddits such as r/politics or r/Conservative.

As a platform designed to sort users based on their interests, Reddit seems the most likely of all the popular social media platforms to cultivate ideologically distinct "echo chambers" in which users are not exposed to cross-cutting news or opinions (McEwan, Carpenter, & Hopke, 2018). The fact that subreddits as ideologically distinct as r/hillaryclinton and r/The_Donald both link to some of the same news sources (e.g., *The Hill* and *Politico*) suggests that Reddit does not sort news consumers into non-overlapping information environments. This is not to say that these subreddits share *all* of their sources with one another. Conservative blogs and websites such as *Breitbart* and *The Daily Caller* are frequently linked to on conservative subreddits but are totally absent from other news or political subreddits. Moreover, reactions to the same news link differ greatly among subreddits.

News consumption on Reddit paints a more complicated picture of the online echo chamber than social theorists and internet scholars anticipated (e.g., Pariser, 2011). Matthew Hindman's (2008) observation that online news audiences are often as concentrated as offline ones around the same large news companies is largely borne out by the data on news sources linked to on Reddit. Major news organizations like *The Guardian* and *The Independent* continue to set the news agenda. Echo chambers on Reddit appear to be asymmetric – evident in some news sources and ideological positions and absent in others. Echo chambers are also not solely a matter of exposure to news sources. The way in which users process and react to the same information, and how those reactions shape other users' reactions, is as important to the formation and maintenance of ideological echo chambers as mere exposure to news content.

Below the surface of popular news subreddits, smaller subreddits discuss news related to specific issues, regions, or groups. In her analysis of a public affairs discussions on r/Seattle, Polly Straub-Cook (2018) found that contributors frequently posted links to niche blogs or directly linked to government documents. This kind of collective curation and discussion of original documents points the way toward something resembling true citizen journalism. At a time when local news continues to suffer from a decades-long decline in revenue (Hendrickson, 2019), this kind of grassroots journalism may serve as a viable, non-commercial alternative.

Breaking news

The unique dynamics of breaking or developing news stories – how they are produced and consumed – warrants consideration from any scholar interested in Reddit and news. Before the internet, cable news developed an expectation of an "always-on" news environment that would relay information about important events as they unfolded. Cable news channels delivered unprecedented immediacy and speed in news coverage (Nadler, 2016), often at the expense of accuracy and context (Rosenberg & Feldman, 2008). The temporal nature of broadcast media required producers to fill the airtime between unpredictable bursts of new, relevant information. News talk radio established a template for extended, extemporaneous editorializing to fill hours of airtime. Both news radio and cable news were often highly partisan, their audiences resembling – demographically and ideologically – the distinct groups who subscribe to different news subreddits and political subreddits. The economics of the cable television and radio industries allowed niche news networks and programs to sustain themselves with audiences that were far smaller than those of network television news shows or nationally syndicated newspapers (Dimmick, 2002).

The internet, in particular, masspersonal media such as Twitter and Reddit, broke down the barrier between live news producers and live news consumers. These technologies, in conjunction with mobile phones, allowed for the instantaneous chronicling and broadcasting of multiple first-hand accounts of an event, creating a sense of immersion and intimacy that traditional news coverage could not generate (Papacharissi, 2015). Once widely adopted within a population, they attain an "ambient" quality: ready to broadcast any noteworthy event regardless of when or where it takes place. To get a sense of the difference between traditional television coverage and masspersonal media coverage of a breaking news story, one might compare television coverage of the 2021 siege on the United States Capitol with the first-hand video footage that circulated on popular social media platforms. Live television coverage was limited by the degree to which reporters could safely observe the event, leaving the viewer at a distance from it. First-hand video produced a chaotic, visceral viewing experience. On Reddit, breaking news threads often incorporate both traditional and first-hand citizen reporting.

While Twitter serves chiefly as a means of broadcasting and re-broadcasting live events, Reddit users engage in something closer to "peer information aggregation," sorting through feeds and posts, evaluating claims, and integrating verified information into a cohesive whole (Barzilai-Nahon, 2008; Leavitt & Robinson, 2017; Priya et al., 2019). In posts marked as "breaking," "updating," or "megathread" (an effort to consolidate discussion of an event into a single post and threaded conversation), contributors continually edit the text of their posts, adding sourced information as it becomes available and refining the text for purposes of comprehensibility (Leavitt & Robinson, 2017). Comments add additional information from other sources, and if the information is deemed important and trustworthy by the original poster, this additional information is added to the post text. If information is consistent across multiple established news organizations, posts are often labeled as "verified" by the original poster. In the absence of such consistency, posts are often tagged by moderators in some way that indicates so (e.g., a "rumor" tag). This moderator intervention is another acknowledgment that many Reddit users only see the post title and do not click on the link to view the text or comments.

Conclusion

As the online news industry enters its third decade, the processes of news production and news distribution have never been more separate. While those within the industry continue to report and write most of the headlines and articles that online news consumers see, distribution has largely been crowdsourced. Reddit's constituents, in the words of Anthony Nadler (2016), are "voting in an election for the news agenda" (p. 122), selecting from the limited options provided by a small number of contributors and moderators who have the time and savvyness to post stories that they believe will resonate with those constituents. Reddit directs "flows of attention" (p. 125) to certain articles, mostly from established media sources and, in smaller subreddits, to blogs and topic-specific websites.

On Reddit as on other social media platforms, headlines from established news sources provide what amounts to a free public service: trustworthy information about world events. Reddit's design consolidates these headlines into easily browsable lists, providing a system for sorting them so that headlines that are more likely to be appealing in some way are easier to find. Contributors can give the link to the news story whatever title they see fit to give it. Often, this means taking a headline that had been optimized to lure readers to click on the link and re-writing it as a more straightforward summation of the article (e.g., r/savedyouaclick). It is an efficient way to deliver news, but not one that guarantees the news producers' any kind of compensation.

Reddit's modularity allows for sorting of news consumers as well, often based on their ideologies. News reported by partisan websites may not reach as many Reddit users as news from established mainstream news sources, but it is often consumed within an ideologically homogeneous context that suppresses dissent. These partisan echo chambers, regardless of their size, can have a profoundly destabilizing influence on societies – a reminder for scholars and researchers to study more than just marketshare.

Reddit's quantification and balkanization of news audiences accelerated processes that were already occurring in an attention marketplace where headlines – rather than entire newspapers – competed with one another. Such a marketplace trains reporters and editors to produce headlines and stories that evoke strong emotional reactions, appealing to particular slices of the population. Traditional news sources don't always rank stories by votes or use sophisticated testing and modeling to determine the values of their products; they may believe that any righteous outrage their stories produce is the byproduct of socially responsible reporting. Still, news is produced with an awareness of the desires of a news consuming public in an evolving information marketplace.

The relationship between news producers and their readership or viewership is not unlike the evolution of subreddits. Over time, producers or contributors learn to deliver a dependable signal of quality to their audiences, settling into a formula that maintains room for flexibility and innovation. They stick to a recognizable format and ideology. In both cases, there is a feedback loop between creator and audience. Reddit merely tightened the loop.

Notes

1 https://www.reddit.com/r/reddit.com/comments/87/the_downing_street_memo/
2 https://arrg.ua.edu/how-reddit-grows.html

References

Abramson, J. (2019). *Merchants of truth: The business of news and the fight for facts*. New York: Simon & Schuster.
Allan, S., & Thorsen, E. (Eds.). (2009). *Citizen journalism: Global perspectives (Vol. 1)*. New York: Peter Lang.

An, J., Kwak, H., Posegga, O., & Jungherr, A. (2019, July). Political discussions in homogeneous and cross-cutting communication spaces. In *Proceedings of the international AAAI conference on web and social media* (pp. 68–79). Association for the Advancement of Artificial Intelligence: Munich, Germany.

Barthel, M., Mitchell, A., Asare-Marfo, D., Kennedy, C., & Worden, K. (2020). Measuring News Consumption in a Digital Era. Pew Research Center. https://www.journalism.org/2020/12/08/measuring-news-consumption-in-a-digital-era/

Barzilai-Nahon, K. (2008). Toward a theory of network gatekeeping: A framework for exploring information control. *Journal of the American Society for Information Science and Technology, 59*(9), 1493–1512. https://doi.org/10.1002/asi.20857

Bruns, A. (2005). *Gatewatching: Collaborative online news production.* New York: Peter Lang.

Dimmick, J. W. (2002). *Media competition and coexistence: The theory of the niche.* London: Routledge.

Dor, D. (2003). On newspaper headlines as relevance optimizers. *Journal of Pragmatics, 35*(5), 695–721.

Duguay, P. A. (2021). Read it on Reddit: Homogeneity and ideological segregation in the age of social news. *Social Science Computer Review,* 08944393211001053.

Eady, G., Nagler, J., Guess, A., Zilinsky, J., & Tucker, J. A. (2019). How many people live in political bubbles on social media? Evidence from linked survey and Twitter data. *Sage Open, 9*(1), 2158244019832705.

Grieco, E. (2020). Fast facts about the newspaper industry's financial struggles as McClatchy files for bankruptcy. Pew Research Center. https://www.pewresearch.org/fact-tank/2020/02/14/fast-facts-about-the-newspaper-industrys-financial-struggles/

Hendrickson, C. (2019). Local journalism in crisis: Why America must revive its local newsrooms. Brookings. https://www.brookings.edu/research/local-journalism-in-crisis-why-america-must-revive-its-local-newsrooms/

Hindman, M. (2009). *The myth of digital democracy.* Princeton, NJ: Princeton University Press.

Hoffa, F. (2017). Reddit top domains: The news sources that reddit prefers. Medium. https://hoffa.medium.com/reddit-favorite-sources-the-most-linked-sites-expanded-and-interactive-79070d648573

Holmqvist, K., Holsanova, J., Barthelson, M., & Lundqvist, D. (2003). Reading or scanning? A study of newspaper and net paper reading. In J. Hyona, R. Radach, & H. Deubel (Eds.) *The mind's eye: Cognitive and applied aspects of eye movement research* (pp. 657–670). Amsterdam: Elsevier Science.

Leavitt, A., & Robinson, J. J. (2017). Upvote my news: The practices of peer information aggregation for breaking news on reddit.com. In *Proceedings of the ACM on human-computer interaction, 1*(CSCW), 1–18.

Lee, E. J. (2012). That's not the way it is: How user-generated comments on the news affect perceived media bias. *Journal of Computer-Mediated Communication, 18*(1), 32–45.

Marchal, N. (2020). The polarizing potential of intergroup affect in online political discussions: Evidence from Reddit r/politics. ssrn. https://ssrn.com/abstract=3671497

McChesney, R., & Nichols, J. (2011). *The death and life of American journalism: The media revolution that will begin the world again.* New York: Nation Books.

McEwan, B., Carpenter, C. J., & Hopke, J. E. (2018). Mediated skewed diffusion of issues information: A theory. *Social Media + Society*, *4*(3), 1–14.

Moy, P., Xenos, M. A., & Hess, V. K. (2005). Communication and citizenship: Mapping the political effects of infotainment. *Mass Communication & Society*, *8*(2), 111–131.

Nadler, A. M. (2016). *Making the news popular: Mobilizing US news audiences.* Urbana: University of Illinois Press.

Nir, R., 1993. A discourse analysis of news headlines. *Hebrew Linguistics*, *37*, 23–31.

O'Sullivan, P. B., & Carr, C. T. (2018). Masspersonal communication: A model bridging the mass-interpersonal divide. *New Media & Society*, *20*(3), 1161–1180.

Papacharissi, Z. (2015). *Affective publics: Sentiment, technology, and politics.* Oxford: Oxford University Press.

Pariser, E. (2011). *The filter bubble: How the new personalized web is changing what we read and how we think.* London: Penguin.

Priya, S., Sequeira, R., Chandra, J., & Dandapat, S. K. (2019). Where should one get news updates: Twitter or Reddit. *Online Social Networks and Media*, *9*, 17–29.

Rosenberg, H., & Feldman, C. S. (2008). *No time to think: The menace of media speed and the 24-hour news cycle.* New York: Continuum.

Schramm, W. (1947). Measuring another dimension of newspaper readership. *Journalism Quarterly*, *24*(4), 293–306.

Starr, P. (2004). *The creation of the media: Political origins of modern communication.* New York: Basic Books.

Straub-Cook, P. (2018). Source, Please? A content analysis of links posted in discussions of public affairs on Reddit. *Digital Journalism*, *6*(10), 1314–1332.

Tewksbury, D., & Althaus, S. L. (2000). Differences in knowledge acquisition among readers of the paper and online versions of a national newspaper. *Journalism & Mass Communication Quarterly*, *77*(3), 457–479.

Tewksbury, D., Weaver, A. J., & Maddex, B. D. (2001). Accidentally informed: Incidental news exposure on the World Wide Web. *Journalism & Mass Communication Quarterly*, *78*(3), 533–554.

Thussu, D. K. (2007). *News as entertainment: The rise of global infotainment.* Ann Arbor: The University of Michigan Press.

Tuchman, G. (1978). *Making news.* New York: Free Press.

8 Reddit as a place

r/arcadegames was created on November 16, 2009. Given Reddit's passion for discussing video games and the significant number of users who could fondly remember the early-1980s heyday of video arcades, the subreddit seemed poised to carve out a moderately sized niche in Reddit's growing ecosystem of communities. Posts about arcades still garner tens of thousands of upvotes in 2021,[1] suggesting that the topic has a lasting appeal. Despite these advantages, r/arcadegames never took off. Only a few hundred users subscribe to the subreddit. Periodically, users will wander in and contribute a post, only to receive no comments and few votes. Over r/arcadegames's 11 year history, none of its posts received more than ten upvotes.

Could r/arcadegames's failure have been a case of bad timing? The similarly themed r/arcade was created several months before r/arcadegames, but did not establish any kind of popularity during that time; there was only a single post on the subreddit, with no votes and no comments, during 2009. Perhaps the category of arcade games was too thin a slice of the larger category of video games to sustain its own subreddit. Subreddits dedicated to esoteric topics often achieve at least moderate success, but more often they fall into obscurity, and there seems to be no obvious way to tell the difference between sustainable niches and unsustainable ones other than simply creating subreddits and seeing what happens.

The kind of failure experienced by r/adcadegames is not unusual. In fact, it's the norm. For the past decade, Reddit users have created hundreds of subreddits *every day*, and while many of them are naked attempts to drive Reddit traffic to other sites (often porn sites), plenty of them are like r/arcadegames: apparently earnest, failed attempts to connect or share something with others. Most subreddits never achieve the critical mass of traffic and contributions needed to sustain themselves. Even in more popular subreddits, most comments fail to get

DOI: 10.4324/9781003150800-8

more than a few upvotes. The way subreddits, posts, and comments are sorted on Reddit makes it difficult to notice just how much of its content and discourse fails to inspire engagement. Visitors to Reddit only tend to see the successes while contributors are well acquainted with a reality as old as the internet: it is hard to get strangers to notice you, even harder to get them to care about what you have to say, and harder still to create a space where many of them will gather together, of their own free will, on a semi-regular basis.

In her book *Online communities: Designing usability and supporting sociability*, Jenny Preece provides a framework for fostering engagement in digital spaces (2000). Many of the lessons in Preece's book are still relevant for creators of fledgling subreddits like r/arcadegames that are just trying to get off the ground. Understanding the needs and desires of potential community members and serving those needs and desires is an evergreen principle of good online community design. But a single-minded focus on growth in numbers of users, subscribers, and contributors leaves questions about what to do once it is achieved unanswered (or even unasked). Assuming one is clever, industrious, and lucky enough to create a popular online community, what then? Should administrators or moderators intervene if the community drifts from the creators' original vision? What if the content starts to become unvaried and homogeneous? What if the community becomes increasingly ideologically extreme, drifting away from reality, fomenting violence and hatred?

Empirical studies of the impact of specific features and characteristics of online communities have begun to yield answers to some of these questions. Such studies provide evidence that moderation of some kind seems necessary to keep conversations on-topic and to keep them civil (e.g., Wright, 2009). In a field experiment conducted in the comments sections of several major newspaper websites, articles allowing users to comment anonymously were considerably more uncivil (e.g., more prone to use ethnic slurs and bigoted language) than articles on the same topic that allowed only non-anonymous commenting (Santana, 2014). In another experiment, Soo-Hye Han and colleagues demonstrated that civility begets civility – participants who are initially exposed to civil discourse in a forum are more apt to express themselves in a civil manner than those exposed to uncivil discourse (Han, Brazeal, & Pennington, 2018). An experiment comparing these two effects – the effect of anonymity and the effect of exposure to civil group norms – found that initial exposure to civil discourse norms was the predominant factor behind the cultivation of civil discourse in online forums (Rösner & Krämer, 2016).

Reddit, with its variations in features and norms among subreddits, offers researchers opportunities to analyze the effects of a wide variety of factors on qualities of discourse. One study compared discourse in a heavily moderated subreddit (r/lgbt) with discourse in a lightly moderated subreddit on the same topic (r/ainbow) (Gibson, 2019). The researcher found that comments in the lightly moderated subreddit tended to be more negative and angry while comments in the heavily moderated subreddit were more positive. Other researchers have worked with subreddit moderators to test the efficacy of changes to subreddit rules or how those rules are enforced. Working with moderators of r/science, J. Nathan Matias found that by simply displaying the rules of participation for the subreddit at the top of the comments (rather than in a harder-to-notice sidebar, as was normally the case), newcomer rates of participation and rule compliance increased (Matias, 2019).

But there are broader aspects of Reddit worth considering: how users flow in and out of subreddits and the platform in general (i.e., user migratory patterns); how subreddits adapt over the years. As well-intentioned as experimental studies designed to improve the quality of online discourse are, the long-term impact of their findings depends on the adoption (and retention) of features and practices by users. After all, what difference will it make if researchers or designers implement an experimentally tested feature that ultimately gets little use, or if the feature is used in some way that administrators had not anticipated? The many experimental, micro-level analyses of features and policies are certainly useful for understanding and improving how Reddit and other online communities work, but they should be supplemented with approaches that can take the entire system into account over long stretches of time.

Some of these macro-level analyses of the evolution of Reddit and other online communities reveal what changes in a community's population do to its discourse, content, and voting behavior. The ease with which users may begin participating in a subreddit – by posting, commenting, or voting – makes sudden surges in subreddit participation possible. Moreover, Reddit's highlighting of posts from certain subreddits on its homepage can bring a subreddit to the attention of millions of users all at once. For most of its first 15 years, Reddit assembled a default home page for new or unregistered users, automatically subscribing them to an administrator-curated list of subreddits (i.e., the default subreddits). Whenever a subreddit was added to the list of default subreddits, it would experience a sudden influx of newcomers, giving researchers an opportunity to examine the effects of growth on subreddits.

Zhiyuan Lin and colleagues examined the effects of this sudden influx of new users on ten subreddits, comparing posting, commenting, and voting behavior within the subreddit before and after each subreddit was added to the defaults (Lin et al., 2017). To assess the extent to which constituents objected to the presence of newcomers, they examined the average vote scores of posts and comments before and after the subreddits were added to the defaults. The researchers reasoned that any attempts to change the character of the subreddit with new kinds of posts or comments would be met with an increase in the number of downvotes. They found that vote scores declined in the months immediately after a subreddit is added to the default, suggesting that existing users were indeed expressing a distaste toward the new direction of the subreddit. After a few months, average vote scores of posts and comments recovered and, in some subreddits, exceeded previous levels. This suggests that new contributions were met with some pushback, but that the pushback didn't last.

What exactly is happening to these subreddits as they grow? One possibility is that existing members were dissatisfied at first but then, as time went on, habituated to the new voice of the subreddit. This pattern of behavior – strenuous objection followed by resigned tolerance – should sound familiar to anyone who has redesigned a popular website or platform. Significant changes are rarely welcomed by existing users, but as time goes on, users tend to get wrapped up in social exchanges and forget about the redesign.

Another possibility is that existing users voiced disapproval by downvoting and then gave up on the community and left. Our research team examined this "displacement effect" – when newcomers push out existing users – in r/TwoXChromosomes, a subreddit dedicated to discussions of topics relating or of interest to girls and women that was added to the default subreddits in May 2014 (Panek, Harrison, & Hou, 2019). We found evidence of a small, lasting displacement effect: after the subreddit was added to the defaults, a significant number of existing contributors stopped contributing and did not resume doing so for the year and a half we monitored. This effect differed depending on how long users had been contributing to the subreddit. Looking at commenters by cohort (cohorts being defined by the month when users first commented in r/TwoXChromosomes), we found clearer evidence of displacement among older cohorts. It should be noted that the vast majority of contributors to this and other subreddits do not return to comment after their first contribution. As noted in Chapter 6, most subreddits retain very small cores of loyal contributors and are chiefly composed of a revolving cast of infrequent contributors.

Looking at the users who contribute to a subreddit's content and discourse is one way to judge whether its character or culture changed as a result of growth. Another way to judge such an effect would be to look at the content of what contributors discuss. Lin and his collaborators wondered whether being added to the defaults made discourse in subreddits more "generic," i.e., less linguistically unique and more similar to discourse on the rest of the platform. They found that subreddits maintain their distinct linguistic identities even after a large number of users have joined them.

The finding that rapidly growing subreddits' discourse does not become more generic does not mean that they did not change. Our analysis of discussion topics in r/TwoXChromosomes indicated that while some topics persisted after the influx of newcomers, others were replaced by new ones. Whereas contributors tended to discuss topics relating to appearance or physical qualities before the influx (e.g., "hair," "body," "weight"), they tended to talk more about topics relating to motherhood afterward (e.g., "mother," "children").

Lin and colleagues also found that after a subreddit is added to the defaults, its contributors comment on a smaller proportion of the subreddit's posts. This would indicate that new subscribers do not evenly distribute their attention across posts, tending instead to cluster around a few popular posts. Such a finding bears out Ferdinand Tönnies's concerns about the effects of the massification of societies on their cultures (Tönnies et al., 1887/2001). What once were conversations become competitions for attention, not because of any particular qualities of newcomers but because of their number.

Such studies only scratch the surface of what we might learn about the ways in which growth – that pillar of the entrepreneurial ethos that undergirds Reddit and every other popular social platform of the early 21st century – affects expressions and behaviors. Conjectures about growth's effects on the characters and functioning of communities are certainly not limited to the outcomes of attention and participation in discourse. In the previous chapters of this book, I have used established theories and empirical research to make the case that the size of a subreddit, and of Reddit in general, can change nearly everything about it: how users present themselves; how public opinion is expressed, quantified, and perceived; how "community" is defined; what kind of news circulates across the world. Rather than limit our perspective to a particular facet or domain, perhaps it is useful when considering the effects of growth to look at Reddit as if it were a place, one not so different from the places in which humans have gathered for thousands of years.

Reddit as a city

Reddit is more place-like, more of a bustling destination than other popular social media platforms. While Facebook hosts relatively small groups of people who are typically acquainted with one another in offline life and Twitter, Instagram, and YouTube connect asymmetric clusters of interest-based groups via the acts of following or subscribing, subreddits are places for large groups to congregate, to talk, to observe one another in relative anonymity. Its users move freely from subreddit to subreddit, some as tourists, some as vandals, and some as residents who are heavily invested in the wellbeing of their community.

When asked what plans he had for the future of Reddit, Reddit's CEO at the time, Yishan Wong, compared Reddit to a city-state.[2] In addition to the physical infrastructure and legal framework that municipalities possess, Wong pointed out that there are less technical, more "human" aspects to them: their communities, institutions, and cultures. The question of how these two components of communal life – the structural and the cultural – influence one another should sound familiar to sociologists and urban planners. And the complaints registered by long-time subscribers and contributors about the "changing character" of Reddit should sound familiar to anyone who has lived in a rapidly gentrifying neighborhood.

From our 21st-century perspective, the fears of urbanization held by many early sociologists seem overblown. Cities have become magnets for talent; they are cultural and academic epicenters as well as economic ones. The chaos many early critics perceived in urban life reflected their inability to understand emerging patterns of behavior. If we could look beyond the physical city blocks and buildings and observe the circulations of people, commerce, and ideas, we would begin to understand how cities truly work, how they create order from diversity, spontaneously generating unprecedented levels of innovation, interdependence, and integration (Webber, 1999).

But if fears of the city were overblown, perhaps its virtues are as well. Cities are often praised for the ways in which they facilitate a mixing of cultures and perspectives, as well as chance encounters that inspire creativity and innovation. But how much interaction or mixing is really going on in cities? Even in networked societies, urban social networks are still affected by physical features such as highway overpasses and rivers, resulting in persistent economic and cultural segregation (Tóth et al., 2021). Sorting and segregating into homogenous groups defeat the purpose of a city that brings people from diverse backgrounds into close physical proximity to one another. It can seem as though any instance of large community – be it the coffeehouse culture of 18th-century Europe, the flourishing cities of the 21st century, or Reddit – isn't really a community when you look at it closely enough.

In the case of physical spaces like cities, differences are often caused and managed by design. The design of physical spaces facilitates or frustrates the abilities of different peoples to congregate, to form connections, to see one another. Online spaces like Reddit and other social media platforms are, of course, also designed. Just as in physical spaces, certain design brings about certain social outcomes, which in turn inform subsequent iterations of design.

Designing for publicness and privacy, for encounters across boundaries of class and ideology and for safe spaces and isolation, are choices faced by both urban planners and online community designers. In her influential treatise on urban life, Jane Jacobs writes about the way planned urban communities in United States in the 1950s attempted to push people into shared, public spaces, forcing them to choose between sharing all their personal lives with others or retreating to their apartments and sharing nothing at all (Jacobs, 1961, p. 66). A venue with a lack of privacy – where everyone knows everyone else's business – is ripe for gossip and drama, and many simply don't want to run the risk of becoming "entangled" in their neighbors' personal affairs. This has the effect of driving away many people who, in a more flexible environment, would be happy to help one another and be socially engaged with strangers. Online, spaces in which people are known to one another – where they have reputations that trail them and are part of a relatively small social circle, like a school or business – are like this: the fear of such "entanglements" often drives people to share very little of their experiences and perspectives.

A certain level of anonymity in urban neighborhoods, Jacobs notes, can maintain a level of accountability while not having the cooling effect on interactions that the threat of gossip and drama create. The neighborhood sidewalk is public in the sense that it is not free from surveillance; residents engage in self-policing behavior, calling out bad behavior and, if necessary, intervening. However, if the city is large enough and the neighborhood porous enough, people will not necessarily know one another and would not go to the trouble of maintaining a record of individuals' bad or good behavior unless it was repeated or egregious.

Reddit allows for this kind of semi-public-ness. A user can go to a subreddit and pose a question that may have caused their relatives or co-workers on Facebook to wonder and worry about them, or may have been retweeted and widely mocked on Twitter. Many subreddits are large enough that gossip and drama, though possible, are unlikely because of how hard it would be to keep track of individuals and their behavior. At the same time, bad behavior that takes place in view of other Reddit "residents" can be collectively censured through downvotes.

Readers looking for examples of such a dynamic are encouraged to seek out popular posts on r/AskReddit relating to mental health. Such posts often garner thousands of comments, with the most visible posts offering concise, compassionate advice grounded in personal experience. More revealing are the replies to comments, which often number in the hundreds and splinter into extended exchanges among multiple contributors. Strangers point one another to specific support subreddits (e.g., r/stopdrinking), offer up their own life stories, and debate the efficacy of institutional support organizations. Downvoting pushes mean, unproductive replies and failed attempts at humor to the bottom of the threads. These intimate, fleeting interactions among strangers are what make Reddit feel "urban" in the best sense of the word.

The same design elements that allow for these kinds of exchanges enable the formation of what an urban planner might think of as "warrens": densely populated, insular enclaves within the larger city (Rao, 2010). For every prosocial exchange on r/AskReddit, there is a mutually reinforced resentment toward others percolating within a smaller subreddit. This makes places that encourage circulation of users among subreddits – what urbanists might think of as plazas or parks – an important counterweight to individualization and fragmentation. In addition to the massively interactive r/AskReddit, r/popular and r/all are analogous to urban "mixed use" spaces, bringing different people, topics, and communities together in one place. As with public parks, Reddit administrators and moderators must decide how much they are willing to let the people decide how space is used. How do you keep the space from becoming too homogeneous? If it becomes overrun by those who pose a threat (or are perceived to pose a threat) to public safety, when and how do you intervene?

One key difference between the urban and digital contexts is the degree to which design – continuous planning and intervention – is accepted by members of the community; not acceptance of a *particular* design but acceptance of *the very idea of a designed community*. The continual re-designing of cities and states is accompanied by a continual debate over *how* the redesign should go – what should be preserved or changed, what changes should be made – but typically not *whether or not* the spaces should be the product of design. In many 21st-century cities, urban planners and designers function as a kind of bulwark protecting the people from unchecked expansion of corporations and businesses, not unlike the position Reddit's administrators and moderators find themselves in, trying to stem the endless tide of spam and self-promotion.

Online, the design of social spaces induces a kind of squeamishness or outright repulsion. In the realm of speech and ideas, any kind of design is perceived as an imposition that is, at best, arbitrary – as evidenced by opaque, ever-changing algorithms that unify fluid online publics – and, at worst, authoritarian – as evidenced by the platforms' creators who are inevitably pilloried as power-hungry ideologues. Freedom is expected in all forms and on all levels of online discourse; structure and design are impositions on that freedom.

With its modular structure, Reddit's social space is more designed than those of other popular social platforms. Each subreddit comes with moderator-approved policies and functions, and the subreddits are embedded in a structure designed and maintained by administrators. Just as the governance that generates and re-generates a city or state's structure is a site of continuous debate and conflict, so too are the policies and moderation of subreddits and Reddit as a whole. While some of the design still comes from administrators who tweak the front page algorithm, much of it comes from a continually refreshed group of Reddit users – the moderators. Entering the online space of Reddit, one tacitly agrees to exist in a structured social environment that is continually re-designed by its users.

Growing up

Social media platforms that rely on user-generated content to create value move through phases: creating growth, sustaining growth, managing growth. Growth is necessary to turn a profit (often a very large one) but it creates what economists might call "externalities," ones that can benefit or harm societies. In the larger history of masspersonal technologies, Reddit's first 15 years may be part of a "wild west" stage of online life in which growth and speed took precedence over order. Such stages are often followed by the implementation of rules and mechanisms that improve the functioning of the system to such a degree that they quickly become taken for granted, making the chaos and unfettered freedom of the earlier stages seem like a distant memory.

Consider the evolution of automobile travel in the early 20th century, from a largely ungoverned system that resulted in many pedestrian deaths and the costly allocation of police labor to direct traffic to an automated traffic-control infrastructure and a set of regulatory laws by which drivers must abide. The management of automobile travel is far from perfect, unevenly distributed across the globe, and many drivers still bristle at or entirely ignore the rules, but the idea that driving is subject to rules of some kind is largely accepted.

As Reddit's administrators and moderators decide how growth should be managed, they would do well to distinguish among the ways in which growth of a subreddit, or Reddit generally, could affect some quality of its character or discourse. The first concerns the raw number of participants: regardless of the characteristics of participants, some outcomes such as conflict or content homogeneity may be a consequence of group size. There may be a linear relationship between group size and these outcomes or there may be a certain threshold of size that, when surpassed, results in a change.

Group size affects the likelihood that any kind of extreme behavior, good or bad, will be observed within a group. Take a small enough sample of humanity and you are unlikely to observe anyone who is extraordinarily wonderful or horrible; take a large enough sample, and you are guaranteed to observe at least a few examples of each. Nothing about the manner in which the people gathered together is responsible for this; their likelihood of inclusion is simply a function of the size of the group. In this way, as Reddit or any subreddit has grown, it becomes more apt to include examples of abhorrent or laudable behaviors or beliefs.

The second way relates to some characteristics of new entrants. A group may grow and its character and discourse may remain fundamentally unchanged until it takes on a group that possesses a particular characteristic, such as a lack of internet savvy or a specific life experience. Here again, the change may be linearly related to the extent of the presence of this group (for every newcomer who possess a particular characteristic, the outcome changes a particular amount) or it may be a matter of a threshold or tipping point (once newcomers possessing a particular characteristic make up more than 50% of the subreddit, the outcome in question changes).

Third, there may be some effect relating to relationships among subreddit constituents or contributors that is a consequence of growth. If growth were to occur among like-minded individuals, regardless of what the group collectively believed or what their life experiences were, the community might not change in any drastic way. But when this group takes on enough new members who possess some different perspective, belief, or experience, the quality of discourse and the character of the community changes. These changes are not due to any particular qualities of the old or the new participants, but rather are a consequence of the relationship between the two. Growth of a community – whether a city, a company, a country, or a social media platform – if it goes far enough, will produce a community that encompasses people with differences; not just demographic differences but differences in experiences, values, and beliefs.

Understanding the effects of growth of Reddit and its subreddits through the years provides scholars and researchers with a new view of collective humanity, one that may help us answer lingering questions about how large communities work. Is the conflict that accompanies growth a product of nativism whereby existing users resent newcomers because they threaten to pollute their pure culture, or a symptom of elitism whereby growth threatens to disturb a delicate balance of power that happens to privilege those defending it? Are groups of a certain size destined to come into irreconcilable conflict with one another, or are there some methods of conflict prevention and resolution that will permit near infinite growth? Is there some developmental stage at which groups, having gone through a requisite period of overt conflicts, mergers, and acquisition, settle into a kind of benign neglect or ignorance of one another? What plays out on Reddit – the walls that growth runs up against, the points at which accord and tolerance fray – may provide clues to the answers to these questions as they play out on other platforms, and as they play out in all social contexts, online and offline.

Notes

1 https://www.reddit.com/r/gaming/comments/ntxfkq/my_husband_is_so_proud_of_his_little_80s_arcade/
2 https://www.reddit.com/r/IAmA/comments/sk1ut/iam_yishan_wong_the_reddit_ceo/c4en44e/?utm_source=reddit&utm_medium=web2x&context=3

References

Gibson, A. (2019). Free speech and safe spaces: How moderation policies shape online discussion spaces. *Social Media+ Society*, *5*(1), 1–15.

Han, S. H., Brazeal, L. M., & Pennington, N. (2018). Is civility contagious? Examining the impact of modeling in online political discussions. *Social Media + Society*, *4*(3), 2056305118793404.

Jacobs, J. (1961). *The death and life of great American cities*. New York: Random House.
Lin, Z., Salehi, N., Yao, B., Chen, Y., & Bernstein, M. S. (2017, May). Better when it was smaller? Community content and behavior after massive growth. In *Eleventh International AAAI conference on web and social media*. Association for the Advancement of Artificial Intelligence: Montreal, Quebec.
Matias, J. N. (2019). Preventing harassment and increasing group participation through social norms in 2,190 online science discussions. *Proceedings of the National Academy of Sciences*, *116*(20), 9785–9789.
Panek, E., Harrison, W., & Hou, J. (2019). Change by default: Exploring the effects of a sudden influx of newcomers on the discourse of r/TwoXChromosomes. *First Monday*, *24*(10).
Preece, J. (2000). *Online communities: Designing usability, supporting sociability*. Chichester: John Wiley & Sons.
Rao, V. (2010). Warrens, plazas and the edge of legibility. Ribbonfarm. https://www.ribbonfarm.com/2010/10/27/warrens-plazas-and-the-edge-of-legibility/
Rösner, L., & Krämer, N. C. (2016). Verbal venting in the social web: Effects of anonymity and group norms on aggressive language use in online comments. *Social Media + Society*, *2*(3), 1–13.
Santana, A. D. (2014). Virtuous or vitriolic: The effect of anonymity on civility in online newspaper reader comment boards. *Journalism Practice*, *8*(1), 18–33.
Tönnies, F., Geuss, R., Hollis, M., & Skinner, Q. (1887/2001). *Tönnies: Community and civil society*. Cambridge: Cambridge University Press.
Tóth, G., Wachs, J., Di Clemente, R., Jakobi, Á., Ságvári, B., Kertész, J., & Lengyel, B. (2021). Inequality is rising where social network segregation interacts with urban topology. *Nature Communications*, *12*(1), 1–9.
Webber, M. (1999). Order in diversity: Community without propinquity. In L. Wingo Jr. (Ed.), *The American cities and technology reader: Wilderness to wired city* (pp. 23–56). Baltimore, MD: The Johns Hopkins Press.
Wright, S. (2009). The role of the moderator: Problems and possibilities for government-run online discussion forums. In P. Gangadharan & T. Davies (Eds.) *Online deliberation: Design, research, and practice* (pp. 233–242). Stanford, CA: Center for the Study of Language and Information.

Index

Note: Page numbers followed by "n" denote endnotes.

For Product Safety Concerns and Information please contact our EU representative GPSR@taylorandfrancis.com Taylor & Francis Verlag GmbH, Kaufingerstraße 24, 80331 München, Germany

Printed and bound by CPI Group (UK) Ltd, Croydon, CR0 4YY
14/09/2026
02216243-0009